CEH Certified Ethical Hacker Certification

The Ultimate Study Guide to Practice Questions and Master the Exam

Table of Contents

Introduction

We are going to embark on a transformative journey into the world of Certified Ethical Hacking, guiding you through a comprehensive set of practice tests designed to equip you with the knowledge, skills, and confidence needed to ace the CEH exam.

Ethical hacking, a critical discipline in cybersecurity, demands a deep understanding of offensive security strategies, tools, and techniques. The CEH certification stands as a testament to one's prowess in understanding vulnerabilities, identifying potential risks, and safeguarding systems through ethical means. This certification validates your ability to think like a hacker while maintaining an ethical approach to protect organizations from malicious cyber threats.

Our aim in this book is simple yet profound: to support your CEH exam preparation by providing an extensive collection of practice test questions. Each question has been meticulously crafted to reflect the complexity and diversity of topics covered in the CEH curriculum. These questions, accompanied by detailed answers and explanations, serve as a powerful tool to reinforce your understanding of the subject matter.

As you immerse yourself in these practice tests, you will encounter scenarios resembling real-world hacking challenges. Through these challenges, you will develop a keen eye for vulnerabilities, learn to navigate various penetration testing methodologies, and fortify your grasp on crucial concepts such as intrusion detection, network security, cryptography, and more.

What sets this book apart is its holistic approach. Not only does it offer practice questions meticulously aligned with the CEH exam objectives, but it also provides insightful explanations and references to relevant study materials. Whether you're a novice eager to venture into the world of ethical hacking or a seasoned professional aiming to validate your expertise, this book serves as an indispensable resource on your journey to CEH certification success.

Throughout these pages, you will discover:

A diverse array of practice questions covering every domain outlined in the CEH exam blueprint.

Detailed explanations and rationales for each question, enabling you to comprehend the underlying principles and methodologies.

Tips, strategies, and insights gleaned from experienced cybersecurity professionals to enhance your exam-taking skills and boost confidence.

Supplementary resources and references to further expand your knowledge base and reinforce your understanding of critical CEH concepts.

By engaging with the content in this book, you are not merely preparing for an exam; you are honing your skills as an ethical hacker. Each question tackled, each concept mastered, brings you one step closer to achieving your goal of becoming a Certified Ethical Hacker.

Join us on this enriching journey as we delve into the intricacies of ethical hacking, unlocking the secrets to success in the CEH certification exam. Let's embark together on the path to mastering the art of ethical hacking and ensuring a safer digital landscape for organizations worldwide.

Chapter 1: Introduction to Ethical Hacking

Ethical hacking stands as the vanguard in the realm of cybersecurity, embodying the paradoxical role of a digital guardian and a master strategist of vulnerabilities. In this chapter, we embark on a foundational journey, unveiling the essence of ethical hacking and its pivotal role in safeguarding the integrity of digital infrastructure.

Ethical hacking, often termed as penetration testing or white-hat hacking, involves the methodical exploration of systems, networks, and applications with the intention of identifying vulnerabilities and weaknesses. This pursuit is not driven by malicious intent but rather by an ethical imperative to fortify security defenses against potential threats.

The Ethical Hacker's Code

Central to the ethos of ethical hacking is a stringent code of conduct. Ethical hackers abide by a set of principles that prioritize integrity, legality, and confidentiality. Their actions are governed by an unwavering commitment to lawful and ethical practices, ensuring that their endeavors serve the purpose of fortifying security rather than compromising it.

Ethical Hacking in Practice

The primary objective of an ethical hacker is to anticipate and preempt cyber threats by adopting the mindset of a potential attacker. By mimicking the strategies and techniques employed by malicious hackers, ethical hackers uncover vulnerabilities before they can be exploited, thus empowering organizations to proactively mitigate risks.

Ethical hacking encompasses a diverse array of methodologies, including but not limited to reconnaissance, scanning, enumeration, exploitation, and post-exploitation. Each phase of this process is meticulously orchestrated, leveraging both automated tools and manual techniques to comprehensively assess the security posture of a system or network.

The Certified Ethical Hacker (CEH) certification is a globally recognized accreditation that validates an individual's proficiency in ethical hacking methodologies, tools, and best practices. It serves as a benchmark for professionals seeking to demonstrate their expertise in this domain, emphasizing the importance of ethical conduct in cybersecurity.

The CEH examination evaluates candidates on a wide spectrum of topics, spanning from reconnaissance and network scanning to system hacking, cryptography, and beyond. Mastery of these domains is essential for aspirants aiming to secure the CEH certification and contribute meaningfully to the cybersecurity landscape.

Ethical hackers serve as the guardians of digital integrity, leveraging their expertise to identify vulnerabilities, fortify defenses, and ensure a safer digital landscape for individuals and organizations alike.

Vulnerability

Vulnerability refers to a weakness in a system's design, implementation, or configuration that can be exploited by attackers. These vulnerabilities can exist in software, hardware, or human factors and can range from coding errors and misconfigurations to flawed security policies. Identifying and addressing vulnerabilities is crucial in maintaining robust cybersecurity posture.

Attack

An attack is an intentional, unauthorized attempt to breach the security measures of a system or network. Attackers exploit vulnerabilities to gain unauthorized access, steal sensitive information, disrupt services, or compromise the integrity of data. Understanding different attack vectors and their potential impact is fundamental in designing effective defense mechanisms.

Security vs. Functionality and Ease of Use

Balancing security with functionality and ease of use is a perpetual challenge in cybersecurity. While stringent security measures might bolster protection, they can sometimes impede user experience or limit functionality. Striking the right balance involves implementing robust security measures without unduly compromising the usability or functionality of systems or applications.

Phases of an Attack

1. Reconnaissance

The initial phase involves gathering information about the target, which may include identifying potential vulnerabilities, system configurations, and network infrastructure.

2. Scanning

In this phase, attackers use various tools and techniques to probe the target network or system for vulnerabilities. This involves port scanning, vulnerability scanning, and enumeration to identify potential entry points.

3. Gaining Access

Exploiting the identified vulnerabilities, attackers attempt to gain unauthorized access to the system or network. This phase involves employing different tactics, such as exploiting weak passwords or leveraging software vulnerabilities.

4. Maintaining Access

Once access is gained, attackers aim to maintain their presence within the system or network. They might create backdoors or establish persistent access to continue their activities undetected.

5. Covering Tracks

To evade detection, attackers cover their tracks by erasing logs, deleting traces of their activities, and obscuring evidence of their unauthorized access.

Types of Hacker Attacks

1. Denial-of-Service (DoS) and Distributed Denial-of-Service (DDoS)

These attacks overwhelm systems or networks with a flood of traffic, causing service disruption by exhausting resources or bandwidth.

2. Malware Attacks

Malicious software, such as viruses, worms, Trojans, and ransomware, is designed to infiltrate systems, steal data, or cause damage.

3. Phishing Attacks

Phishing involves tricking individuals into revealing sensitive information, often through deceptive emails or websites, to gain unauthorized access or compromise data.

4. Man-in-the-Middle (MitM) Attacks

These attacks intercept communication between two parties, allowing attackers to eavesdrop, manipulate, or steal information.

SQL Injection and Other Code Exploitation

By injecting malicious code into applications or databases, attackers exploit vulnerabilities to access or manipulate data.

Understanding these facets of vulnerability, attack methodologies, and the diverse landscape of hacker attacks is critical in formulating robust defense strategies and safeguarding against potential threats in the ever-evolving cybersecurity landscape.

Hacktivism

Hacktivism involves the use of hacking techniques and tools to promote social or political causes. Unlike traditional hacking aimed at personal gain or disruption, hacktivism focuses on advocating for specific ideologies or bringing attention to social issues. However, the legality and ethics of hacktivism remain debated, as it often involves unauthorized access to systems or data.

Ethical Hackers

Ethical hackers, also known as white-hat hackers, are cybersecurity professionals who use hacking skills and techniques for legitimate and lawful purposes. Their primary goal is to identify vulnerabilities, assess security measures, and strengthen defenses within ethical boundaries. They play a crucial role in fortifying systems and networks by proactively identifying weaknesses before malicious hackers exploit them.

Vulnerability Research

Vulnerability research involves the systematic exploration and analysis of software, hardware, or systems to uncover potential security weaknesses. Researchers aim to discover and report vulnerabilities responsibly to the relevant parties, such as software developers or vendors, allowing for timely patches or fixes to mitigate the risks associated with these vulnerabilities.

Ethical Hacking Assignment

An ethical hacking assignment typically involves conducting authorized security assessments or penetration tests on a system, network, or application. Ethical hackers simulate real-world attack scenarios to identify vulnerabilities and assess the overall security posture. The findings and recommendations from such assignments aid organizations in strengthening their security measures and mitigating potential risks.

Computer Crime

Computer crime encompasses a broad spectrum of illegal activities carried out using computers or computer networks. These crimes include but are not limited to hacking, identity theft, phishing, malware distribution, fraud, and cyber espionage. Law enforcement agencies and cybersecurity professionals work together to investigate, prevent, and prosecute computer crimes to maintain digital safety and security.

Understanding these aspects of cyber activities, ranging from hacktivism and ethical hacking to vulnerability research and the implications of computer crime, is essential in navigating the complex landscape of cybersecurity and fostering a safer digital environment for individuals and organizations.

Practice Questions and Answers

1. What is the primary goal of ethical hacking?

A. To compromise systems for personal gain

B. To identify vulnerabilities and strengthen security

C. To disrupt services and networks

D. To steal sensitive information

Answer: B. To identify vulnerabilities and strengthen security

Explanation: Ethical hacking aims to proactively find weaknesses in systems or networks to bolster defenses. It is about strengthening security rather than exploiting vulnerabilities for personal gain.

2. Which phase of an attack involves gathering information about the target, such as system configurations and network infrastructure?

A. Scanning

B. Gaining Access

C. Reconnaissance

D. Covering Tracks

Answer: C. Reconnaissance

Explanation: Reconnaissance involves collecting information about the target, which is crucial for planning and executing an attack.

3. What is the main objective of vulnerability research?

A. To exploit vulnerabilities for personal gain

B. To identify weaknesses and report them responsibly

C. To create new vulnerabilities in systems

D. To disrupt systems and networks

Answer: B. To identify weaknesses and report them responsibly

Explanation: Vulnerability research aims to find vulnerabilities ethically and report them to the relevant parties for proper mitigation.

4. Which type of attack aims to overwhelm systems with a flood of traffic, causing service disruption?

A. Phishing Attack

B. Man-in-the-Middle Attack

C. Denial-of-Service (DoS) Attack

D. SQL Injection Attack

Answer: C. Denial-of-Service (DoS) Attack

Explanation: DoS attacks flood systems with traffic, rendering them inaccessible to legitimate users.

5. What distinguishes ethical hackers from malicious hackers?

A. Malicious intent and unlawful activities

B. Technical skills and knowledge

C. Employment status in cybersecurity

D. Use of hacking tools

Answer: A. Malicious intent and unlawful activities

Explanation: Ethical hackers operate within legal boundaries and aim to improve security, unlike malicious hackers who engage in unlawful activities for personal gain or disruption.

6. What term describes the use of hacking techniques for social or political causes?

A. Cybercrime

B. Hacktivism

C. Malware

D. Phishing

Answer: B. Hacktivism

Explanation: Hacktivism involves using hacking skills to advocate for social or political causes.

7. Which phase of an attack involves erasing logs and obscuring evidence of unauthorized access?

A. Gaining Access

B. Scanning

C. Covering Tracks

D. Maintaining Access

Answer: C. Covering Tracks

Explanation: Covering Tracks is the phase where attackers try to hide their presence to evade detection.

8. What does a man-in-the-middle attack involve?

A. Intercepting communication between two parties

B. Flooding a system with traffic

C. Injecting malicious code into a website

D. Stealing sensitive information through email

Answer: A. Intercepting communication between two parties

Explanation: A man-in-the-middle attack involves intercepting and possibly altering communication between two parties without their knowledge.

9. What is the primary focus of an ethical hacking assignment?

A. To exploit vulnerabilities for personal gain

B. To disrupt services and networks

C. To conduct unauthorized penetration tests

D. To identify vulnerabilities and strengthen security

Answer: D. To identify vulnerabilities and strengthen security

Explanation: Ethical hacking assignments aim to uncover vulnerabilities within a system or network and provide recommendations to enhance security measures.

10. What term describes the deliberate attempt to trick individuals into revealing sensitive information?

A. Phishing

B. Malware

C. DoS Attack

D. Reconnaissance

Answer: A. Phishing

Explanation: Phishing involves deceiving individuals to divulge sensitive information through deceptive means like emails or fake websites.

11. What distinguishes a Distributed Denial-of-Service (DDoS) attack from a Denial-of-Service (DoS) attack?

A. DDoS attacks use multiple systems to target a single network

B. DoS attacks are more sophisticated and harder to detect

C. DDoS attacks involve phishing techniques

D. DoS attacks target hardware exclusively

Answer: A. DDoS attacks use multiple systems to target a single network

Explanation: DDoS attacks involve multiple systems coordinated to overwhelm a target, whereas DoS attacks come from a single source.

12. What characterizes a SQL injection attack?

A. Flooding a system with traffic

B. Intercepting communication between parties

C. Injecting malicious code into a database query

D. Exploiting weak passwords

Answer: C. Injecting malicious code into a database query

Explanation: SQL injection involves inserting malicious SQL code into input fields to manipulate databases.

13. Which action is a primary responsibility of ethical hackers?

A. Exploiting vulnerabilities for personal gain

B. Reporting identified vulnerabilities responsibly

C. Hiding vulnerabilities to test security measures

D. Disrupting services to assess system resilience

Answer: B. Reporting identified vulnerabilities responsibly

Explanation: Ethical hackers discover vulnerabilities and report them to the appropriate authorities or organizations for proper mitigation.

14. What is the primary focus of vulnerability research?

A. Creating new vulnerabilities in systems

B. Identifying weaknesses and reporting them responsibly

C. Exploiting vulnerabilities for personal gain

D. Disrupting services to test system security

Answer: B. Identifying weaknesses and reporting them responsibly

Explanation: Vulnerability research aims to find weaknesses and report them ethically to improve overall security.

15. What best describes the goal of an ethical hacking assignment?

A. To exploit as many vulnerabilities as possible

B. To disrupt services and networks for testing purposes

C. To identify vulnerabilities and recommend security improvements

D. To impersonate users to test system access controls

Answer: C. To identify vulnerabilities and recommend security improvements

Explanation: Ethical hacking assignments aim to identify vulnerabilities and suggest ways to enhance security measures.

16. Which type of attack involves tricking individuals into revealing sensitive information by impersonating a trustworthy entity?

A. DoS Attack

B. Man-in-the-Middle Attack

C. Phishing Attack

D. SQL Injection Attack

Answer: C. Phishing Attack

Explanation: Phishing involves deceptive tactics to trick individuals into divulging sensitive information.

17. What distinguishes ethical hackers from malicious hackers?

A. Employment status in cybersecurity

B. Technical skills and knowledge

C. Use of hacking tools

D. Intent and actions

Answer: D. Intent and actions

Explanation: Ethical hackers work within legal boundaries to improve security, while malicious hackers engage in unlawful activities for personal gain or disruption.

18. Which phase of an attack involves probing a target system or network for vulnerabilities?

A. Gaining Access

B. Scanning

C. Reconnaissance

D. Covering Tracks

Answer: B. Scanning

Explanation: Scanning involves using various tools to probe for vulnerabilities in a target system or network.

19. What is the primary goal of ethical hacking?

A. To compromise systems for personal gain

B. To identify vulnerabilities and strengthen security

C. To disrupt services and networks

D. To steal sensitive information

Answer: B. To identify vulnerabilities and strengthen security

Explanation: Ethical hacking aims to proactively identify vulnerabilities and enhance security measures.

20. What term describes the deliberate attempt to intercept communication between two parties?

A. Phishing

B. Man-in-the-Middle Attack

C. DoS Attack

D. Reconnaissance

Answer: B. Man-in-the-Middle Attack

Explanation: A man-in-the-middle attack involves intercepting and possibly altering communication between two parties.

21. Which phase of an attack involves exploiting identified vulnerabilities to gain unauthorized access?

A. Scanning

B. Gaining Access

C. Covering Tracks

D. Reconnaissance

Answer: B. Gaining Access

Explanation: Gaining Access involves exploiting vulnerabilities to gain unauthorized entry into a system or network.

22. What characterizes a Denial-of-Service (DoS) attack?

A. Intercepting communication between two parties

B. Flooding a system with traffic to disrupt services

C. Injecting malicious code into a database query

D. Exploiting weak passwords

Answer: B. Flooding a system with traffic to disrupt services

Explanation: DoS attacks overwhelm systems with traffic, making services inaccessible to legitimate users.

23. Which action best represents the primary focus of vulnerability research?

A. Exploiting vulnerabilities for personal gain

B. Reporting identified vulnerabilities responsibly

C. Hiding vulnerabilities to test security measures

D. Disrupting services to assess system resilience

Answer: B. Reporting identified vulnerabilities responsibly

Explanation: Vulnerability research involves finding weaknesses and responsibly reporting them for mitigation.

24. What distinguishes a Distributed Denial-of-Service (DDoS) attack from a Denial-of-Service (DoS) attack?

A. DDoS attacks target hardware exclusively

B. DoS attacks use multiple systems to target a single network

C. DDoS attacks involve phishing techniques

D. DoS attacks are more sophisticated and harder to detect

Answer: B. DDoS attacks use multiple systems to target a single network

Explanation: DDoS attacks coordinate multiple systems to overwhelm a target, while DoS attacks originate from a single source.

25. What characterizes a SQL injection attack?

A. Flooding a system with traffic

B. Intercepting communication between parties

C. Injecting malicious code into a database query

D. Exploiting weak passwords

Answer: C. Injecting malicious code into a database query

Explanation: SQL injection involves inserting malicious SQL code into input fields to manipulate databases.

26. Which action is a primary responsibility of ethical hackers?

A. Exploiting vulnerabilities for personal gain

B. Reporting identified vulnerabilities responsibly

C. Hiding vulnerabilities to test security measures

D. Disrupting services to assess system resilience

Answer: B. Reporting identified vulnerabilities responsibly

Explanation: Ethical hackers find vulnerabilities and report them for proper mitigation.

27. What is the primary focus of vulnerability research?

A. Creating new vulnerabilities in systems

B. Identifying weaknesses and reporting them responsibly

C. Exploiting vulnerabilities for personal gain

D. Disrupting services to test system security

Answer: B. Identifying weaknesses and reporting them responsibly

Explanation: Vulnerability research aims to find weaknesses and report them ethically for better security.

28. What best describes the goal of an ethical hacking assignment?

A. To exploit as many vulnerabilities as possible

B. To disrupt services and networks for testing purposes

C. To identify vulnerabilities and recommend security improvements

D. To impersonate users to test system access controls

Answer: C. To identify vulnerabilities and recommend security improvements

Explanation: Ethical hacking assignments aim to find vulnerabilities and suggest ways to improve security measures.

29. Which type of attack involves tricking individuals into revealing sensitive information by impersonating a trustworthy entity?

A. DoS Attack

B. Man-in-the-Middle Attack

C. Phishing Attack

D. SQL Injection Attack

Answer: C. Phishing Attack

Explanation: Phishing uses deceptive tactics to trick individuals into disclosing sensitive information.

30. What distinguishes ethical hackers from malicious hackers?

A. Employment status in cybersecurity

B. Technical skills and knowledge

C. Use of hacking tools

D. Intent and actions

Answer: D. Intent and actions

Explanation: Ethical hackers work within legal boundaries to improve security, while malicious hackers engage in unlawful activities for personal gain or disruption.

Chapter 2: Footprinting and Reconnaissance/Scanning Networks

Footprinting involves the systematic gathering of information about a target system, network, or organization. This critical phase aims to comprehensively map out the digital footprint of the target, identifying potential entry points and vulnerabilities.

A myriad of methodologies and techniques are employed during Footprinting. These include passive information gathering through publicly available sources, active scanning, DNS interrogation, and social engineering tactics to assemble a detailed profile of the target.

Reconnaissance serves as the precursor to probing deeper into the target network. It involves discovering network hosts, services, and vulnerabilities through methods such as network scanning, port scanning, and OS fingerprinting.

Network scanning encompasses various methodologies to map out the network topology, identify active hosts, and unveil potential vulnerabilities. Tools such as Nmap and Nessus aid in this process, offering insights crucial for subsequent phases of penetration testing.

Understanding Footprinting and Reconnaissance is integral to the Certified Ethical Hacker (CEH) certification. Mastery of these phases is essential for CEH candidates, as it forms the bedrock for subsequent assessments and penetration testing methodologies.

The practical application of Footprinting and Reconnaissance extends beyond certification exams. Ethical hackers utilize these skills to uncover security flaws, assist in security assessments, and fortify organizations against potential cyber threats.

Footprinting and Reconnaissance are the keystones in ethical hacking, representing the meticulous groundwork necessary for comprehensive security evaluations. Embracing the methodologies and techniques outlined in this chapter equips aspiring ethical hackers with the tools needed to dissect and fortify digital fortresses against potential vulnerabilities.

Information Gathering Methodology

Archived Websites

Archived websites, like the Wayback Machine, retain historical data about websites, providing valuable insights into changes, content, and potential vulnerabilities across different time frames.

Search Public Records

Utilizing publicly available records allows for the collection of information about organizations, individuals, or entities, aiding in the assessment of potential security risks.

Tools

Various tools such as Maltego, Shodan, or theHarvester automate the information gathering process by aggregating data from different sources, streamlining reconnaissance efforts.

Locating the Network Range

Determining the network range assists in identifying active hosts and potential entry points within a targeted network.

Conducting Active and Passive Reconnaissance Against a Target

Passive Reconnaissance

Gathering information without directly interacting with the target, often involving analyzing public information or social engineering tactics to construct a profile without alerting the target.

Active Reconnaissance

Interacting directly with the target system or network to obtain information, which might involve scanning ports, querying DNS servers, or probing network devices for details.

Scanning Networks

Scanning Methodology

Involves various scanning techniques such as ping sweeps, port scans, and OS detection, providing insights into active hosts, services, and potential vulnerabilities.

Three-Way Handshake

The fundamental process in establishing a TCP connection, involving SYN, SYN-ACK, and ACK packets exchanged between client and server.

TCP Flags

Flags within TCP packets (SYN, ACK, FIN, RST, PSH, URG) convey specific instructions and statuses during communication, crucial for understanding network behavior.

Types of Port Scans

Different port scan types (TCP Connect, SYN, UDP, etc.) offer varying degrees of stealth and detail in uncovering open ports and services on a target system.

Using Nmap and Zenmap

Nmap

A powerful, open-source tool for network exploration and security auditing, offering diverse scanning capabilities and robust scripting for customized assessments.

Zenmap

The graphical interface for Nmap, providing a user-friendly approach to visualize and interpret Nmap's scanning results.

Crafting Packets and Scanning Countermeasures

Crafting Packets

Developing specialized packets for specific tasks, such as bypassing firewall rules or testing network defenses.

Scanning Countermeasures

Measures implemented by organizations to thwart scanning attempts, including firewalls, intrusion detection systems (IDS), and intrusion prevention systems (IPS).

Understanding these components equips ethical hackers with the methodology, tools, and knowledge essential for effective information gathering, reconnaissance, and scanning while navigating potential countermeasures.

Practice Questions and Answers

1. What is the primary purpose of Footprinting in ethical hacking?

A. Gaining unauthorized access to systems

B. Gathering comprehensive information about a target

C. Exploiting vulnerabilities immediately

D. Testing network security tools

Answer: B. Gathering comprehensive information about a target

Explanation: Footprinting involves systematically collecting information about a target system or network to assess its security posture.

2. Which method involves gathering information about a target without directly interacting with it?

A. Active reconnaissance

B. Scanning networks

C. Passive reconnaissance

D. Conducting port scans

Answer: C. Passive reconnaissance

Explanation: Passive reconnaissance involves collecting information without directly engaging with the target system or network.

3. What is the purpose of conducting active reconnaissance?

A. To gather information without alerting the target

B. To interact directly with the target for information gathering

C. To exploit vulnerabilities immediately

D. To disrupt services and networks

Answer: B. To interact directly with the target for information gathering

Explanation: Active reconnaissance involves directly engaging with the target system or network to obtain information.

4. Which tool is commonly used for automated information gathering and reconnaissance?

A. Maltego

B. Wayback Machine

C. Nessus

D. Zenmap

Answer: A. Maltego

Explanation: Maltego is a tool that automates information gathering and reconnaissance by aggregating data from various sources.

5. What does TCP/IP three-way handshake involve?

A. Establishing a secure connection between two parties

B. Sending data packets in a loop to verify connectivity

C. Initiating a denial-of-service attack

D. Establishing a TCP connection through SYN, SYN-ACK, and ACK packets

Answer: D. Establishing a TCP connection through SYN, SYN-ACK, and ACK packets

Explanation: The TCP three-way handshake is a process for establishing a TCP connection between a client and a server.

6. Which flag in a TCP packet is used to initiate a connection?

A. RST

B. SYN

C. ACK

D. FIN

Answer: B. SYN

Explanation: The SYN flag in a TCP packet is used to initiate a connection.

7. What is the purpose of port scanning during network reconnaissance?

A. To establish secure connections

B. To identify active hosts and open ports

C. To create denial-of-service attacks

D. To exploit vulnerabilities

Answer: B. To identify active hosts and open ports

Explanation: Port scanning helps in identifying active hosts and the services running on them.

8. Which port scanning technique sends a complete TCP connection request to the target?

A. SYN Scan

B. ACK Scan

C. UDP Scan

D. TCP Connect Scan

Answer: D. TCP Connect Scan

Explanation: TCP Connect Scan involves establishing a full TCP connection to the target ports.

9. Which tool is used for network scanning and security auditing?

A. Wireshark

B. Nikto

C. Nmap

D. Metasploit

Answer: C. Nmap

Explanation: Nmap is a widely used tool for network scanning and security auditing.

10. What is the graphical interface for Nmap, providing a user-friendly way to visualize scanning results?

A. Nikto

B. Metasploit

C. Zenmap

D. Wireshark

Answer: C. Zenmap

Explanation: Zenmap is the graphical interface for Nmap, facilitating a user-friendly visualization of scanning results.

11. Which phase of ethical hacking involves systematically gathering historical data about websites?

A. Active Reconnaissance

B. Passive Reconnaissance

C. Scanning Networks

D. Archived Websites

Answer: D. Archived Websites

Explanation: Archived websites retain historical data, aiding in understanding changes and potential vulnerabilities over time.

12. What information gathering method involves accessing publicly available records?

A. Archived Websites

B. Search Public Records

C. Tools

D. Locating the Network Range

Answer: B. Search Public Records

Explanation: Accessing publicly available records aids in collecting information about entities or organizations.

13. What technique aids in determining the network range of a target?

A. Archived Websites

B. Search Public Records

C. Tools

D. Locating the Network Range

Answer: D. Locating the Network Range

Explanation: Locating the network range helps identify potential hosts and entry points within the network.

14. What distinguishes passive reconnaissance from active reconnaissance?

A. Passive uses tools, while active involves manual processes

B. Passive interacts directly with the target, while active does not

C. Passive involves direct interaction with the target, while active does not

D. Passive gathers information without alerting the target, while active engages directly

Answer: D. Passive gathers information without alerting the target, while active engages directly

Explanation: Passive reconnaissance gathers information discreetly, whereas active reconnaissance engages with the target system directly.

15. Which TCP flag initiates the termination of a connection?

A. SYN

B. ACK

C. FIN

D. RST

Answer: C. FIN

Explanation: The FIN flag in a TCP packet initiates the termination of an established connection.

16. Which port scanning technique does not complete the full TCP connection process?

A. TCP Connect Scan

B. SYN Scan

C. ACK Scan

D. UDP Scan

Answer: B. SYN Scan

Explanation: SYN Scan does not complete the full TCP connection but initiates it to gather information about open ports.

17. Which tool is known for its capacity to visualize scanning results in a user-friendly manner?

A. Wireshark

B. Metasploit

C. Nikto

D. Zenmap

Answer: D. Zenmap

Explanation: Zenmap provides a graphical interface for Nmap's scanning results, making it more user-friendly.

18. What action involves developing specialized packets for specific tasks during reconnaissance?

A. Scanning Methodology

B. Crafting Packets

C. Three-Way Handshake

D. TCP Flags

Answer: B. Crafting Packets

Explanation: Crafting packets involves creating specialized packets for specific reconnaissance tasks.

19. What are scanning countermeasures used for in network security?

A. To bypass firewalls

B. To create vulnerabilities

C. To thwart scanning attempts

D. To exploit weaknesses

Answer: C. To thwart scanning attempts

Explanation: Scanning countermeasures are implemented to prevent or detect scanning attempts by attackers.

20. Which port scanning technique sends a TCP ACK packet to identify filtered ports?

A. SYN Scan

B. ACK Scan

C. UDP Scan

D. FIN Scan

Answer: B. ACK Scan

Explanation: ACK Scan sends TCP ACK packets to identify filtered ports, which are neither open nor closed.

21. What is the primary objective of conducting reconnaissance in ethical hacking?

A. To exploit vulnerabilities immediately

B. To interact directly with the target for information gathering

C. To gather information without alerting the target

D. To disrupt services and networks

Answer: C. To gather information without alerting the target

Explanation: Reconnaissance aims to gather information discreetly without raising suspicion or alerting the target.

22. Which information gathering method involves using tools to automate the collection of data from various sources?

A. Archived Websites

B. Search Public Records

C. Tools

D. Locating the Network Range

Answer: C. Tools

Explanation: Tools automate the collection of data from various sources, streamlining the reconnaissance process.

23. What technique aids in determining the range of IP addresses within a network?

A. Archived Websites

B. Search Public Records

C. Tools

D. Locating the Network Range

Answer: D. Locating the Network Range

Explanation: Locating the network range helps identify potential hosts and entry points within the network.

24. What distinguishes active reconnaissance from passive reconnaissance?

A. Active uses tools, while passive involves manual processes

B. Active interacts directly with the target, while passive does not

C. Active involves direct interaction with the target, while passive does not

D. Active gathers information without alerting the target, while passive engages directly

Answer: C. Active involves direct interaction with the target, while passive does not

Explanation: Active reconnaissance involves directly engaging with the target system or network to obtain information.

25. Which TCP flag acknowledges the successful receipt of data packets?

A. SYN

B. ACK

C. FIN

D. RST

Answer: B. ACK

Explanation: The ACK flag in a TCP packet acknowledges the successful receipt of data packets.

26. Which port scanning technique sends packets with the FIN flag to identify open ports?

A. TCP Connect Scan

B. SYN Scan

C. ACK Scan

D. FIN Scan

Answer: D. FIN Scan

Explanation: FIN Scan sends packets with the FIN flag to identify open ports on a target system.

27. Which tool is widely used for network reconnaissance and vulnerability scanning?

A. Wireshark

B. Metasploit

C. Nmap

D. Nikto

Answer: C. Nmap

Explanation: Nmap is extensively used for network reconnaissance and vulnerability scanning.

28. What action involves developing specialized packets to manipulate network devices during reconnaissance?

A. Scanning Methodology

B. Crafting Packets

C. Three-Way Handshake

D. TCP Flags

Answer: B. Crafting Packets

Explanation: Crafting packets involves creating specialized packets to manipulate network devices for reconnaissance purposes.

29. What are scanning countermeasures primarily used for in network security?

A. To evade detection by intrusion detection systems

B. To create vulnerabilities for ethical hackers

C. To exploit weaknesses in network protocols

D. To prevent or detect scanning attempts

Answer: D. To prevent or detect scanning attempts

Explanation: Scanning countermeasures are implemented to thwart or identify scanning attempts by attackers.

30. Which port scanning technique sends UDP packets to identify open ports?

A. SYN Scan

B. ACK Scan

C. UDP Scan

D. FIN Scan

Answer: C. UDP Scan

Chapter 3: Enumeration

Enumeration is a crucial phase in ethical hacking that involves extracting detailed information about a target network or system post-reconnaissance. This process significantly aids in identifying potential vulnerabilities and weak points that could be exploited.

Steps to Compromise a System

1. Service Discovery

Purpose: Identify active services, their versions, and configurations.

Tools: Tools like NetBIOS, SNMP, or LDAP queries can reveal running services and their configurations.

2. User Enumeration

Purpose: Acquire information about users, their roles, privileges, and potential entry points.

Methods: Utilize tools like User Enumeration Scripts or Protocol-Specific Queries (e.g., LDAP queries) to gather user-related data.

3. Network Enumeration

Purpose: Map out network topology, identify hosts, open ports, and active connections.

Techniques: Use tools like Netstat, Nmap, or Network Sniffers to scrutinize network traffic and map the network layout.

4. Operating System Enumeration

Purpose: Discover the target system's OS type, version, and potential vulnerabilities.

Methods: Employ tools like OS Fingerprinting tools or Banner Grabbing techniques to glean OS information.

5. File and Share Enumeration

Purpose: Identify accessible files, directories, and shared resources.

Approaches: Leverage tools like SMBclient or NFS tools to list available shares and files on networked systems.

Relevance in Ethical Hacking

Understanding Enumeration provides ethical hackers with a detailed blueprint of a target system or network. This comprehensive knowledge is pivotal for crafting tailored attack strategies, mitigating vulnerabilities, and fortifying system defenses.

Ethical Implications

Ethical hackers must conduct Enumeration with a strict adherence to legal and ethical boundaries. The acquired information should solely be used for enhancing security and not for malicious intent or unauthorized access.

Enumeration is a critical phase that bridges reconnaissance and exploitation. It equips ethical hackers with profound insights into system configurations, user privileges, and network architecture, enabling them to strengthen defenses and protect against potential cyber threats. Ethical usage of these techniques ensures the fortification of systems rather than their compromise.

Enumeration

Enumeration, a critical phase in ethical hacking, involves systematically extracting detailed information from a target system or network post-reconnaissance. It focuses on acquiring specifics about users, services, shares, network resources, and configurations to identify potential vulnerabilities for further exploitation.

NetBIOS Basics

Purpose of NetBIOS

NetBIOS (Network Basic Input/Output System) is an API that enables communication between devices in a LAN. It assists in identifying resources, such as shares, users, and computers, and facilitates their interaction within a network.

Role in Enumeration

NetBIOS, with its suite of commands and protocols, can aid in extracting valuable information during enumeration. It helps identify network shares, active machines, and available services.

Command-Line Tools

Enumeration Tools in Command Line

Nbtstat: This Windows command-line tool allows querying NetBIOS over TCP/IP.

Net Commands: Various 'Net' commands in Windows, like 'Net User' or 'Net View', retrieve user and share information.

Enum4Linux: A Linux-based tool that focuses on enumerating information from Samba (SMB) shares, aiding in user and group enumeration.

Use Cases of Command-Line Tools

Nbtstat: Obtain NetBIOS information about remote machines, such as the NetBIOS name table, local cache statistics, or registered adapter status.

Net Commands: Retrieve user account information, share details, and network information from Windows-based systems.

Enum4Linux: Extract user and share information, gather group membership details, and perform robust enumeration against Samba shares.

Significance in Ethical Hacking

Understanding and utilizing command-line tools for enumeration, particularly those that interact with NetBIOS, enhances an ethical hacker's ability to gather vital information without alerting the target. This data, acquired ethically, helps bolster system defenses and rectify vulnerabilities.

Enumeration, bolstered by NetBIOS basics and adept usage of command-line tools, forms a pivotal stage in ethical hacking. Mastery of these tools and protocols aids ethical hackers in comprehensively assessing potential entry points, user privileges, and system configurations, empowering them to fortify networks against potential cyber threats.

SNMP Enumeration

Purpose of SNMP

SNMP (Simple Network Management Protocol) is utilized to manage devices on an IP network. It allows network administrators to monitor and manage network devices, collect information, and modify device configurations.

Role in Enumeration

In the context of enumeration, SNMP can be leveraged to extract valuable information such as system details, device configurations, running services, and potentially sensitive data if the SNMP community strings are not secured properly.

Discovering Hosts with Windows Command Line Tools

Windows Command-Line Tools for Host Discovery

Windows offers several built-in command-line tools that aid in discovering hosts:

ping: A basic utility that sends ICMP echo requests to ascertain if a host is reachable on the network.

arp: Displays and modifies the ARP cache, assisting in mapping IP addresses to MAC addresses and identifying local devices on the same subnet.

nslookup: Allows querying DNS servers to retrieve information about IP addresses and domain names.

Discovering Hosts with Metasploit

Metasploit Framework

Metasploit, a powerful open-source penetration testing framework, offers modules for various tasks, including host discovery:

ARP Scanner: Conducts ARP scans to discover hosts on the local network.

Ping Sweeps: Utilizes ICMP echo requests to identify live hosts.

Port Scans: Determines open ports on discovered hosts to assess potential vulnerabilities.

Using Cain

Role of Cain

Cain and Abel is a popular security tool used for network analysis. It aids in:

Password Cracking: Decrypting passwords captured through various protocols like ARP, SNMP, FTP, etc.

Man-in-the-Middle (MITM) Attacks: Intercepting network traffic and capturing data packets for analysis.

ARP Poisoning: Manipulating ARP tables to redirect traffic and intercept data between two connected devices.

Ethical Use

It's important to note that while these tools and protocols offer significant insights into network infrastructure and potential vulnerabilities, their ethical use is paramount. Ethical hackers should operate within legal boundaries, ensuring proper authorization before conducting any form of network scanning or probing.

Understanding and effectively utilizing these tools in an ethical manner significantly contributes to a thorough enumeration process, allowing ethical hackers to identify weaknesses, secure networks, and prevent potential security breaches.

Practice Questions and Answers

1. What is the primary purpose of Enumeration in ethical hacking?

A. To exploit vulnerabilities immediately

B. To gather detailed information about a target system

C. To disrupt network services

D. To conduct password cracking

Answer: B. To gather detailed information about a target system

Explanation: Enumeration aims to extract specific information about a system or network post-reconnaissance for potential vulnerabilities.

2. SNMP (Simple Network Management Protocol) is primarily used for:

A. Managing devices on an IP network

B. File sharing in a network

C. Securing network communication

D. Conducting ARP poisoning attacks

Answer: A. Managing devices on an IP network

Explanation: SNMP is a protocol used for managing and monitoring network devices.

3. Which command-line tool in Windows is used for querying DNS servers to retrieve information about IP addresses and domain names?

A. ping

B. arp

C. nslookup

D. netstat

Answer: C. nslookup

Explanation: The nslookup command allows querying DNS servers to retrieve information about IP addresses and domain names.

4. What does ARP (Address Resolution Protocol) primarily assist in doing?

A. Mapping IP addresses to MAC addresses

B. DNS resolution

C. Conducting ping sweeps

D. Port scanning

Answer: A. Mapping IP addresses to MAC addresses

Explanation: ARP helps in mapping IP addresses to MAC addresses within a local network.

5. In Metasploit, what module would you use to conduct an ARP scan to discover hosts on the local network?

A. Ping Sweeps

B. Port Scans

C. ARP Scanner

D. SNMP Enumerator

Answer: C. ARP Scanner

Explanation: The ARP Scanner module in Metasploit is used to conduct ARP scans for discovering hosts on the local network.

6. What role does Cain and Abel serve in network security analysis?

A. Conducting ARP poisoning attacks

B. Preventing network intrusions

C. Managing firewall configurations

D. Encrypting sensitive data

Answer: A. Conducting ARP poisoning attacks

Explanation: Cain and Abel is known for conducting ARP poisoning attacks, among other network analysis functions.

7. What does SNMP stand for in network management?

A. Secure Network Management Protocol

B. Simple Network Management Protocol

C. Systematic Network Monitoring Protocol

D. Standard Network Mapping Protocol

Answer: B. Simple Network Management Protocol

Explanation: SNMP stands for Simple Network Management Protocol, used for managing network devices.

8. Which tool is commonly used for DNS enumeration and reconnaissance?

A. ping

B. arp

C. nslookup

D. netstat

Answer: C. nslookup

Explanation: nslookup is frequently used for DNS enumeration and reconnaissance tasks.

9. What is the primary purpose of using Metasploit in ethical hacking?

A. To conduct ARP poisoning attacks

B. To perform password cracking

C. To conduct penetration tests and vulnerability assessments

D. To manage network firewalls

Answer: C. To conduct penetration tests and vulnerability assessments

Explanation: Metasploit is primarily used for conducting penetration tests, assessing vulnerabilities, and exploiting them ethically.

10. What is the primary aim of ARP scans in network enumeration?

A. Identifying open ports on a target system

B. Discovering hosts on the local network

C. Mapping IP addresses to MAC addresses

D. Conducting ping sweeps

Answer: B. Discovering hosts on the local network

Explanation: ARP scans help in discovering hosts within the local network by mapping IP addresses to MAC addresses.

11. What role does SNMP play in network management?

A. Identifying network shares

B. Managing network devices

C. Conducting password cracking

D. Encrypting network traffic

Answer: B. Managing network devices

Explanation: SNMP (Simple Network Management Protocol) assists in managing network devices by monitoring and controlling their activities.

12. Which command-line tool helps in mapping IP addresses to MAC addresses on a local network?

A. ping

B. arp

C. nslookup

D. netstat

Answer: B. arp

Explanation: The arp command is used to view and modify the ARP cache, mapping IP addresses to MAC addresses in a local network.

13. How does ARP poisoning contribute to network reconnaissance?

A. Encrypts network traffic

B. Helps in DNS resolution

C. Discovers hosts on the local network

D. Redirects network traffic for interception

Answer: D. Redirects network traffic for interception

Explanation: ARP poisoning manipulates the ARP tables to redirect network traffic, allowing for interception and analysis.

14. In Metasploit, what module would you use to conduct a ping sweep to identify live hosts?

A. ARP Scanner

B. Ping Sweeps

C. Port Scans

D. SNMP Enumerator

Answer: B. Ping Sweeps

Explanation: The Ping Sweeps module in Metasploit is used to conduct ping sweeps for identifying live hosts.

15. What is the primary function of Cain and Abel in ethical hacking?

A. Conducting ARP poisoning attacks

B. Intercepting encrypted traffic

C. Preventing network intrusions

D. Managing firewall configurations

Answer: A. Conducting ARP poisoning attacks

Explanation: Cain and Abel is known for conducting ARP poisoning attacks among other network analysis functions.

16. What does DNS enumeration primarily involve?

A. Mapping IP addresses to MAC addresses

B. Resolving IP addresses to domain names

C. Conducting ping sweeps

D. Enumerating SNMP communities

Answer: B. Resolving IP addresses to domain names

Explanation: DNS enumeration involves querying DNS servers to resolve IP addresses to domain names.

17. Which protocol does SNMP stand for in network management?

A. Simple Network Management Protocol

B. Systematic Network Monitoring Protocol

C. Secure Network Management Protocol

D. Standard Network Mapping Protocol

Answer: A. Simple Network Management Protocol

Explanation: SNMP stands for Simple Network Management Protocol used in managing network devices.

18. Which tool is commonly utilized for DNS-related enumeration tasks?

A. ping

B. arp

C. nslookup

D. netstat

Answer: C. nslookup

Explanation: nslookup is frequently used for DNS-related enumeration tasks.

19. What is the primary aim of using Metasploit in ethical hacking?

A. To conduct ARP poisoning attacks

B. To perform password cracking

C. To manage network firewalls

D. To conduct penetration tests and vulnerability assessments

Answer: D. To conduct penetration tests and vulnerability assessments

Explanation: Metasploit is primarily used for conducting penetration tests, assessing vulnerabilities, and exploiting them ethically.

20. What is the primary purpose of conducting ARP scans in network enumeration?

A. Identifying open ports on a target system

B. Discovering hosts on the local network

C. Mapping IP addresses to MAC addresses

D. Conducting ping sweeps

Answer: B. Discovering hosts on the local network

Explanation: ARP scans assist in discovering hosts within the local network by mapping IP addresses to MAC addresses.

21. What's the primary function of SNMP in network management?

A. Secure data transmission

B. Monitoring and managing network devices

C. Firewall configuration

D. Conducting ping sweeps

Answer: B. Monitoring and managing network devices

Explanation: SNMP primarily serves for monitoring and managing network devices.

22. Which command-line tool is used to view and modify the ARP cache?

A. ping

B. arp

C. nslookup

D. netstat

Answer: B. arp

Explanation: The arp command assists in viewing and modifying the ARP cache, mapping IP addresses to MAC addresses on a local network.

23. How does ARP poisoning contribute to network reconnaissance?

A. Encrypts network traffic

B. Resolves DNS queries

C. Discovers hosts on the local network

D. Redirects and intercepts network traffic

Answer: D. Redirects and intercepts network traffic

Explanation: ARP poisoning redirects and intercepts network traffic, facilitating detailed analysis and reconnaissance.

24. Which Metasploit module is used to conduct an ARP scan for discovering hosts on the local network?

A. ARP Scanner

B. Ping Sweeps

C. Port Scans

D. SNMP Enumerator

Answer: A. ARP Scanner

Explanation: The ARP Scanner module in Metasploit is utilized for conducting ARP scans to identify hosts on the local network.

25. What's the primary role of Cain and Abel in ethical hacking?

A. Conducting ARP poisoning attacks

B. Analyzing encrypted traffic

C. Preventing network intrusions

D. Managing network firewalls

Answer: A. Conducting ARP poisoning attacks

Explanation: Cain and Abel specialize in conducting ARP poisoning attacks among other network analysis functions.

26. What does DNS enumeration primarily entail?

A. Mapping IP addresses to MAC addresses

B. Resolving IP addresses to domain names

C. Conducting ping sweeps

D. Enumerating SNMP communities

Answer: B. Resolving IP addresses to domain names

Explanation: DNS enumeration involves querying DNS servers to resolve IP addresses to domain names.

27. Which protocol does SNMP stand for in network management?

A. Simple Network Management Protocol

B. Systematic Network Monitoring Protocol

C. Secure Network Management Protocol

D. Standard Network Mapping Protocol

Answer: A. Simple Network Management Protocol

Explanation: SNMP stands for Simple Network Management Protocol used for managing network devices.

28. Which tool is often used for DNS-related enumeration tasks?

A. ping

B. arp

C. nslookup

D. netstat

Answer: C. nslookup

Explanation: nslookup is commonly employed for DNS-related enumeration tasks.

29. What's the primary purpose of using Metasploit in ethical hacking?

A. To conduct ARP poisoning attacks

B. To perform password cracking

C. To manage network firewalls

D. To conduct penetration tests and vulnerability assessments

Answer: D. To conduct penetration tests and vulnerability assessments

Explanation: Metasploit is primarily used for conducting penetration tests, assessing vulnerabilities, and exploiting them ethically.

30. What's the primary objective of conducting ARP scans in network enumeration?

A. Identifying open ports on a target system

B. Discovering hosts on the local network

C. Mapping IP addresses to MAC addresses

D. Conducting ping sweeps

Answer: B. Discovering hosts on the local network

Explanation: ARP scans assist in discovering hosts within the local network by mapping IP addresses to MAC addresses.

Chapter 4: System Hacking

Passive online attacks involve gathering password-related information without directly interacting with the target system. These attacks focus on capturing data as it moves across the network, aiming to decipher passwords without actively engaging the system or the user.

Password Attack Example

Brute Force Attack

A brute force attack is a common method wherein an attacker systematically tries all possible combinations of passwords until the correct one is found. This method, while straightforward, can be time-consuming and resource-intensive, especially for complex and lengthy passwords.

Null Sessions

Null Sessions

Null sessions are unauthorized connections to Windows systems where an anonymous user connects to the IPC$ share without requiring a password. This access could potentially provide unauthorized information about usernames, groups, and shares on the network.

Relevance in Ethical Hacking

Understanding passive online attacks, like null sessions, and password attack methods, such as brute force attacks, assists ethical hackers in recognizing potential vulnerabilities within systems and networks. Identifying and rectifying these weaknesses helps fortify the security posture of the systems they're protecting.

Ethical Implications

Ethical hackers must use their knowledge responsibly, ensuring they have explicit permission to conduct any form of testing or penetration attempts. Unauthorized access or testing without proper authorization is illegal and unethical.

System hacking involves multiple methods and techniques, including passive online attacks like null sessions and brute force attacks. Ethical hackers utilize these techniques to identify and rectify vulnerabilities, bolstering system defenses against potential intrusions or unauthorized access attempts. Their ethical conduct ensures the enhancement of security measures, protecting systems from malicious attacks.

Kerberos Operation

Kerberos is a network authentication protocol that provides secure authentication for users and services over a non-secure network. Its operation involves three primary components:

Authentication Server (AS): Responsible for initial authentication and issuing Ticket Granting Ticket (TGT).

Ticket Granting Server (TGS): Provides service tickets after receiving TGT.

Client: Requests services using tickets obtained from the TGS.

Kerberos utilizes symmetric key cryptography to securely authenticate users and services without transmitting passwords over the network.

Password Cracking Countermeasures

Strong Password Policies

Implementing strong password policies can mitigate password cracking attempts. This includes enforcing complex passwords, regular password changes, and multi-factor authentication to enhance security.

Encryption and Salting

Storing passwords using strong encryption and adding random salts to them makes password hashes harder to crack even if the hash is obtained by an attacker.

Escalating Privileges

Privilege Escalation

Privilege escalation involves gaining higher access privileges than initially granted. It can be achieved through various means such as exploiting software vulnerabilities, misconfigurations, or weak permissions.

Countermeasures

Regularly updating systems, applying patches, using least privilege principles, and employing proper access controls help prevent privilege escalation.

Password Cracking

Techniques

Password cracking involves various techniques, including dictionary attacks, brute force attacks, and rainbow table attacks to decrypt passwords from hashed data.

Countermeasures

Implementing strong password policies, using robust encryption methods, and employing multi-factor authentication can mitigate the risk of successful password cracking attempts.

Understanding the operation of Kerberos, implementing robust password cracking countermeasures, preventing privilege escalation, and adopting strong security practices contribute significantly to enhancing system security and protecting against unauthorized access and attacks.

Keyloggers

Functionality

Keyloggers are malicious tools designed to capture keystrokes on a system, recording user activities. They can capture sensitive information like passwords, credit card numbers, and other confidential data.

Detection and Prevention

Detecting keyloggers involves using anti-malware software, regularly updating systems, and avoiding suspicious downloads. Prevention includes employing security tools and being cautious with software installations.

Hiding Files

File Concealment Techniques

Hiding files involves methods like changing file attributes (hidden or system files), using file encryption, employing steganography, or utilizing software with file-hiding functionalities.

Detection and Prevention

Detection involves using file exploration tools that reveal hidden files or employing antivirus scans. Prevention requires secure file permissions, regular system checks, and utilizing encryption to protect sensitive data.

Rootkits

Characteristics

Rootkits are malicious software that provide unauthorized access to a system while hiding their presence. They alter system functionalities to evade detection and maintain persistence.

Detection and Prevention

Detection includes using rootkit scanners or anti-rootkit tools that identify unusual system behavior. Prevention involves keeping systems updated, using firewalls, and employing intrusion detection systems.

Steganography

Purpose

Steganography involves concealing messages or data within other innocuous files or mediums like images, audio, or text. This method aims to hide the existence of the communicated information.

Detection and Prevention

Detecting steganography requires specialized tools that analyze file data for hidden content. Prevention involves using encryption, limiting access to sensitive data, and employing strict data transfer policies.

Covering Tracks

Techniques

Covering tracks involves erasing logs, clearing browsing history, deleting temporary files, and using tools that overwrite data remnants to prevent forensic analysis.

Detection and Prevention

Detection involves forensic analysis tools that identify attempts to erase or modify logs. Prevention requires employing secure logging mechanisms and limiting user privileges to prevent tampering.

Understanding these concepts aids in recognizing potential security threats and implementing strategies to mitigate risks, ensuring better protection against unauthorized access and data breaches.

Practice Questions and Answers

1. What is the primary purpose of a keylogger?

A. Capturing keystrokes

B. Encrypting files

C. Deleting system logs

D. Scanning for malware

Answer: A. Capturing keystrokes

Explanation: Keyloggers are designed to capture and record keystrokes, potentially capturing sensitive information.

2. How can files be hidden on a system?

A. Changing file permissions

B. Using file encryption

C. Employing steganography

D. All of the above

Answer: D. All of the above

Explanation: Files can be hidden through various means including changing permissions, encryption, and steganography.

3. What characterizes a rootkit?

A. Conceals its presence

B. Encrypts files

C. Alters system attributes

D. Deletes system logs

Answer: A. Conceals its presence

Explanation: Rootkits hide their presence while providing unauthorized access to a system.

4. What is the primary objective of steganography?

A. Deleting files

B. Hiding information within other files

C. Encrypting data

D. Erasing logs

Answer: B. Hiding information within other files

Explanation: Steganography conceals information within innocuous files or mediums.

5. What are common techniques for covering tracks in cybersecurity?

A. Overwriting data remnants

B. Deleting browsing history

C. Clearing logs

D. All of the above

Answer: D. All of the above

Explanation: Covering tracks involves various techniques like overwriting data, deleting logs, and clearing browsing history.

6. Which cybersecurity threat involves capturing user keystrokes?

A. Rootkit

B. Keylogger

C. Steganography

D. Encryption

Answer: B. Keylogger

Explanation: Keyloggers capture and record user keystrokes.

7. How can files be hidden on a system using steganography?

A. Altering file permissions

B. Encrypting files

C. Concealing data within images or other files

D. Deleting files

Answer: C. Concealing data within images or other files

Explanation: Steganography hides data within seemingly innocuous files or mediums.

8. What is a characteristic of a rootkit?

A. Encrypts files

B. Deletes browsing history

C. Conceals its presence

D. Encrypts network traffic

Answer: C. Conceals its presence

Explanation: Rootkits hide their presence to provide unauthorized access to a system.

9. What's the primary purpose of covering tracks in cybersecurity?

A. Erasing logs and evidence of activities

B. Encrypting files and data

C. Deleting system files

D. Scanning for malware

Answer: A. Erasing logs and evidence of activities

Explanation: Covering tracks involves erasing logs and evidence to prevent forensic analysis.

10. What is the primary function of steganography in cybersecurity?

A. Encrypting files

B. Hiding information within other files or mediums

C. Deleting files

D. Erasing logs

Answer: B. Hiding information within other files or mediums

Explanation: Steganography conceals information within seemingly innocuous files or mediums.

11. What is the primary function of a keylogger in cybersecurity?

A. Encrypting data

B. Capturing and recording keystrokes

C. Deleting system logs

D. Erasing browsing history

Answer: B. Capturing and recording keystrokes

Explanation: Keyloggers are designed to capture and record keystrokes made by users on a system.

12. How can files be hidden using steganography?

A. Changing file extensions

B. Encrypting file contents

C. Concealing data within images or other files

D. Renaming files

Answer: C. Concealing data within images or other files

Explanation: Steganography hides data within seemingly innocuous files or mediums like images or text files.

13. What defines a rootkit in cybersecurity?

A. Encrypts files on the system

B. Conceals its presence from detection

C. Alters system configurations

D. Deletes browsing history

Answer: B. Conceals its presence from detection

Explanation: Rootkits hide their presence to provide unauthorized access without detection.

14. Which technique involves hiding messages or information within other files or media?

A. Encryption

B. Steganography

C. Keylogging

D. File Compression

Answer: B. Steganography

Explanation: Steganography involves concealing information within seemingly innocent files or media.

15. What is a common method used for covering tracks in cybersecurity?

A. Encrypting log files

B. Overwriting data remnants

C. Deleting system files

D. Scanning for malware

Answer: B. Overwriting data remnants

Explanation: Overwriting data remnants is a method used for covering tracks and preventing forensic analysis.

16. Which cybersecurity threat captures user input, such as passwords and sensitive data?

A. Keylogger

B. Rootkit

C. Steganography

D. Encryption

Answer: A. Keylogger

Explanation: Keyloggers capture and record user keystrokes, including sensitive information.

17. How can files be hidden using steganography techniques?

A. Renaming file extensions

B. Changing file permissions

C. Concealing data within other files or mediums

D. Compressing files

Answer: C. Concealing data within other files or mediums

Explanation: Steganography hides data within seemingly innocuous files or mediums.

18. What defines a rootkit in cybersecurity terms?

A. Encrypts network traffic

B. Conceals its presence

C. Deletes system logs

D. Encrypts files

Answer: B. Conceals its presence

Explanation: Rootkits hide their presence to provide unauthorized access without detection.

19. What is the primary objective of covering tracks in cybersecurity?

A. Encrypting files

B. Concealing information within files

C. Erasing logs and evidence of activities

D. Deleting system files

Answer: C. Erasing logs and evidence of activities

Explanation: Covering tracks involves erasing logs and evidence to prevent forensic analysis.

20. What's the primary purpose of steganography in cybersecurity?

A. Hiding malware within files

B. Encrypting data

C. Concealing information within other files or mediums

D. Deleting files

Answer: C. Concealing information within other files or mediums

Explanation: Steganography conceals information within seemingly innocuous files or mediums.

21. What is the primary function of a keylogger in cybersecurity?

A. Encrypting data

B. Capturing and recording keystrokes

C. Deleting system logs

D. Erasing browsing history

Answer: B. Capturing and recording keystrokes

Explanation: Keyloggers are designed to capture and record keystrokes made by users on a system.

22. How can files be hidden using steganography?

A. Changing file extensions

B. Encrypting file contents

C. Concealing data within images or other files

D. Renaming files

Answer: C. Concealing data within images or other files

Explanation: Steganography hides data within seemingly innocuous files or mediums like images or text files.

23. What defines a rootkit in cybersecurity?

A. Encrypts files on the system

B. Conceals its presence from detection

C. Alters system configurations

D. Deletes browsing history

Answer: B. Conceals its presence from detection

Explanation: Rootkits hide their presence to provide unauthorized access without detection.

24. Which technique involves hiding messages or information within other files or media?

A. Encryption

B. Steganography

C. Keylogging

D. File Compression

Answer: B. Steganography

Explanation: Steganography involves concealing information within seemingly innocent files or media.

25. What is a common method used for covering tracks in cybersecurity?

A. Encrypting log files

B. Overwriting data remnants

C. Deleting system files

D. Scanning for malware

Answer: B. Overwriting data remnants

Explanation: Overwriting data remnants is a method used for covering tracks and preventing forensic analysis.

26. Which cybersecurity threat captures user input, such as passwords and sensitive data?

A. Keylogger

B. Rootkit

C. Steganography

D. Encryption

Answer: A. Keylogger

Explanation: Keyloggers capture and record user keystrokes, including sensitive information.

27. How can files be hidden using steganography techniques?

A. Renaming file extensions

B. Changing file permissions

C. Concealing data within other files or mediums

D. Compressing files

Answer: C. Concealing data within other files or mediums

Explanation: Steganography hides data within seemingly innocuous files or mediums.

28. What defines a rootkit in cybersecurity terms?

A. Encrypts network traffic

B. Conceals its presence

C. Deletes system logs

D. Encrypts files

Answer: B. Conceals its presence

Explanation: Rootkits hide their presence to provide unauthorized access without detection.

29. What is the primary objective of covering tracks in cybersecurity?

A. Encrypting files

B. Concealing information within files

C. Erasing logs and evidence of activities

D. Deleting system files

Answer: C. Erasing logs and evidence of activities

Explanation: Covering tracks involves erasing logs and evidence to prevent forensic analysis.

30. What's the primary purpose of steganography in cybersecurity?

A. Hiding malware within files

B. Encrypting data

C. Concealing information within other files or mediums

D. Deleting files

Answer: C. Concealing information within other files or mediums

Explanation: Steganography conceals information within seemingly innocuous files or mediums.

Chapter 5: Trojans, Backdoors, Viruses, and Worms

Trojan horses are malicious software disguised as legitimate programs. They appear harmless but contain malicious code that can execute unauthorized activities on a system, such as stealing sensitive data, creating backdoors for attackers, or causing system damage.

Indicators of a Trojan Attack

Signs of Trojan Infection

Unexpected Behavior: Unusual or unexpected behavior from the system, such as frequent crashes or slow performance.

Unsolicited Pop-ups: Sudden appearance of unwanted pop-ups or advertisements during regular use.

Unauthorized Access: Suspicious access to sensitive files, folders, or applications without user intervention.

Strange Network Activity: Unexplained network traffic or unusual data transfers without user action.

Relevance in Cybersecurity

Understanding Trojan horses and their potential indicators helps in identifying and mitigating attacks. Employing robust antivirus software, firewalls, and regularly updating systems can prevent Trojan infections.

Trojan horses, although disguised as harmless software, can cause significant harm to systems and networks. Recognizing their indicators and implementing stringent security measures are vital for protecting against these deceptive and damaging cyber threats.

Ports Used by Trojans

Trojan Ports

Trojans often use various ports for communication. Some commonly used ports include:

Port 21 (FTP): Used by FTP Trojans.

Port 23 (Telnet): Exploited by Telnet Trojans.

Port 80 (HTTP): Employed by HTTP-based Trojans.

Port 666 (Doom): Associated with Doom or Back Orifice Trojans.

Port 1433 (SQL): Used by SQL-based Trojans.

Netstat Command

Netstat Usage

The netstat command in networking provides information about network connections, routing tables, interface statistics, and more. It displays active TCP/IP connections, ports, and listening services.

Types of Trojans

Trojan Variants

Remote Access Trojans (RATs): Allow unauthorized remote access to systems.

Data Sending Trojans: Transmit sensitive data to unauthorized recipients.

Destructive Trojans: Cause damage by deleting or corrupting files.

Proxy Trojans: Redirect traffic through compromised systems.

ICMP Tunneling

ICMP Tunneling

ICMP (Internet Control Message Protocol) tunneling involves encapsulating data within ICMP packets. Attackers use this method to bypass firewalls or filters by transmitting data covertly.

Tools Used to Create Trojans

Trojan Creation Tools

Trojan Development Kits: e.g., Poison Ivy, Beast, etc.

Backdoor Generators: e.g., Back Orifice, NetBus, SubSeven, etc.

Remote Access Tools: e.g., DarkComet, ProRAT, etc.

Trojan Countermeasures

Mitigating Trojan Threats

Firewalls: Filter and block suspicious traffic.

Antivirus Software: Detect and remove Trojan infections.

Regular Updates: Patch vulnerabilities and keep systems updated.

Safe Practices: Avoid downloading from untrusted sources and be cautious with email attachments.

Understanding the ports used by Trojans, leveraging network monitoring commands like netstat, recognizing various Trojan types, understanding ICMP tunneling risks, being aware of tools used to create Trojans, and implementing robust countermeasures are crucial in combating and mitigating Trojan threats.

Detecting Tools

Trojan Detection Tools

Antivirus Software: Detects known Trojan signatures and behaviors.

Intrusion Detection Systems (IDS): Monitors network traffic for suspicious activities.

Rootkit Detectors: Identify hidden processes and files associated with Trojans.

Backdoor Countermeasures

Mitigating Backdoors

Regular Security Audits: Conduct audits to detect and close vulnerabilities.

Firewalls: Configure to block unauthorized access and outgoing connections.

Hardening Systems: Secure configurations, patch regularly, and restrict unnecessary services.

Countermeasure Tools

Tools for Countering Threats

Firewalls: Examples include pfSense, iptables, Windows Firewall, etc.

Intrusion Detection/Prevention Systems (IDPS): e.g., Snort, Suricata, etc.

Security Auditing Tools: Like Nessus, OpenVAS, etc.

Process Monitor

Functionality

Process Monitor is a Windows tool used for monitoring system activities, such as file system, registry, and process/thread activity. It helps in troubleshooting and identifying malicious processes or suspicious activities.

Malware Tool: Poison Ivy

Poison Ivy

Poison Ivy is a remote administration tool used for unauthorized access and control of compromised systems. It allows attackers to execute commands, steal data, and control the victim's machine remotely.

Understanding detection tools like antivirus software and IDS, implementing backdoor countermeasures through regular audits and firewall configurations, employing various countermeasure tools like firewalls and IDPS, utilizing process monitoring tools like Process Monitor, and being aware of malware tools like Poison Ivy are crucial aspects in fortifying systems against cyber threats.

Viruses and Worms

Symptoms of a Virus

Slow System Performance: Unexplained slowdowns in system speed or responsiveness.

Unexpected Behavior: Unexpected pop-ups, crashes, or unusual error messages.

Missing or Corrupted Files: Files disappearing or becoming corrupted without user action.

Stages of a Virus' Life

Dormant Stage: The virus remains inactive, hidden, and doesn’t spread.

Propagation Stage: The virus spreads to other programs or systems.

Triggering Stage: Activation through a trigger event or condition.

Execution Stage: The virus performs intended actions, causing damage or replicating.

Infection Phase

Infection Phase

During this phase, viruses attach themselves to host programs or files and execute malicious actions when these infected files are accessed or run.

Types of Viruses

File Infector Viruses: Infect executable files.

Macro Viruses: Infect document files that contain macros.

Boot Sector Viruses: Infect the boot sector of storage devices.

Polymorphic Viruses: Change their code to avoid detection.

What Viruses Attack

Viruses can target various elements:

Files: Infect executable or data files.

Boot Sector: Infect the boot sector of storage devices.

Networks: Spread through network connections.

Applications: Target specific software vulnerabilities.

Understanding the symptoms of viruses, the lifecycle stages of a virus, the infection phase, different types of viruses, and their target elements are crucial in identifying, preventing, and mitigating the impact of these malicious programs on systems and networks.

How Viruses Infect

Infection Methods

Email Attachments: Sent as attachments in emails, often exploiting user interaction to execute.

Infected Files: Downloading or executing infected files from the internet or removable media.

Drive-by Downloads: Automatic downloads from compromised websites.

Networks: Spreading through vulnerable network connections.

Self-Modification Viruses

Self-Modifying Viruses

Self-modifying viruses change their code or appearance to avoid detection by antivirus programs. They alter their structure or encrypt their content to evade detection mechanisms.

The Worst Computer Viruses

Notorious Viruses

ILOVEYOU (Love Bug): Spread via email, causing widespread damage.

Melissa Virus: Propagated through email, infecting documents.

Sasser Worm: Exploited Windows vulnerabilities, causing system crashes.

File Extensions

File Extensions and Viruses

File extensions, like .exe, .doc, or .xls, represent the type of file and can be targeted by viruses. Viruses often disguise themselves as legitimate files by using these extensions.

Countermeasures

Measures to Combat Viruses

Antivirus Software: Regularly updated to detect and remove viruses.

Firewalls: Filter incoming and outgoing network traffic.

User Awareness: Educate users about safe browsing habits and avoiding suspicious downloads.

Regular Backups: Ensure data backup to recover from virus-induced damage.

Understanding how viruses infect systems, the evasion techniques of self-modifying viruses, being aware of notorious viruses' impact, recognizing file extensions that can harbor viruses, and implementing robust countermeasures are essential in safeguarding systems against these threats.

Antivirus Software

Functionality

Antivirus software detects, prevents, and removes malicious software (malware) from computers. It scans files, emails, and web traffic, identifying and eliminating viruses, worms, Trojans, and other threats.

Utilizing Malware

Malware Utilization

Malicious actors use malware for various purposes:

Data Theft: Stealing sensitive information like passwords or financial data.

System Disruption: Causing system crashes or disabling functionalities.

Remote Access: Gaining unauthorized control over compromised systems.

Financial Gain: Extorting money through ransomware or conducting fraud.

Exploiting the Connection

Exploiting Connections

Attackers exploit various connections to propagate malware:

Emails: Sending infected attachments or links.

Internet: Drive-by downloads from compromised or malicious websites.

Networks: Exploiting vulnerabilities in network connections for propagation.

Understanding the functionality of antivirus software, recognizing the utilization of malware for malicious purposes, and being aware of the exploitation of various connections by attackers are essential in mitigating the risks associated with cyber threats.

Practice Questions and Answers

1. What characterizes a Trojan horse?

A. It replicates itself

B. It conceals its presence

C. It requires user interaction to execute

D. It spreads through network connections

Answer: C. It requires user interaction to execute

Explanation: Trojan horses masquerade as legitimate software and require user intervention to execute.

2. Which port is commonly associated with FTP Trojans?

A. Port 21

B. Port 23

C. Port 80

D. Port 666

Answer: A. Port 21

Explanation: FTP Trojans often utilize port 21, the standard port for FTP (File Transfer Protocol).

3. What is a common indicator of a virus infection?

A. Slow system performance

B. Unauthorized network access

C. Hardware failure

D. Regular system updates

Answer: A. Slow system performance

Explanation: Virus infections can cause system slowdowns and unexpected behavior.

4. What characterizes the propagation stage of a virus' life?

A. It spreads to other programs or systems

B. It remains hidden and inactive

C. It activates through a trigger event

D. It performs malicious actions

Answer: A. It spreads to other programs or systems

Explanation: During the propagation stage, the virus spreads to infect other programs or systems.

5. What is a self-modifying virus known for?

A. Stealing sensitive information

B. Encrypting its code to avoid detection

C. Causing system crashes

D. Spreading through email attachments

Answer: B. Encrypting its code to avoid detection

Explanation: Self-modifying viruses change their code or structure to evade detection.

6. Which file extension is commonly targeted by viruses?

A. .exe

B. .txt

C. .jpg

D. .mp3

Answer: A. .exe

Explanation: Viruses often target executable (.exe) files to infect systems.

7. What is a primary function of antivirus software?

A. Sending spam emails

B. Monitoring system performance

C. Detecting and removing malware

D. Encrypting files

Answer: C. Detecting and removing malware

Explanation: Antivirus software detects and removes malicious software from systems.

8. How do attackers often propagate malware through networks?

A. By encrypting files

B. Through drive-by downloads

C. By sending phishing emails

D. By disabling firewalls

Answer: B. Through drive-by downloads

Explanation: Attackers spread malware by initiating automatic downloads from compromised websites.

9. What is a common purpose of utilizing malware by malicious actors?

A. Improving system performance

B. Gaining unauthorized access

C. Providing system security

D. Enhancing network speed

Answer: B. Gaining unauthorized access

Explanation: Malicious actors often use malware to gain unauthorized access to systems.

10. Which type of malware requires user interaction to execute?

A. Worm

B. Virus

C. Trojan

D. Backdoor

Answer: C. Trojan

Explanation: Trojans masquerade as legitimate software and require user interaction to execute.

11. How does a backdoor differ from a Trojan?

A. Backdoors require user interaction

B. Trojans provide unauthorized access

C. Backdoors spread independently

D. Trojans self-replicate

Answer: B. Trojans provide unauthorized access

Explanation: Trojans provide unauthorized access while disguising themselves as legitimate software.

12. Which type of malware spreads independently, exploiting vulnerabilities?

A. Virus

B. Backdoor

C. Trojan

D. Worm

Answer: D. Worm

Explanation: Worms spread independently, exploiting system vulnerabilities to propagate.

13. What phase of a virus' life involves remaining hidden and inactive?

A. Propagation stage

B. Execution stage

C. Dormant stage

D. Triggering stage

Answer: C. Dormant stage

Explanation: The dormant stage involves the virus remaining inactive and hidden.

14. What is a primary characteristic of a self-modifying virus?

A. Replicates quickly

B. Encrypts its code to avoid detection

C. Requires user interaction to spread

D. Infects only specific file types

Answer: B. Encrypts its code to avoid detection

Explanation: Self-modifying viruses change their code or structure to evade detection.

15. Which extension is commonly targeted by macro viruses?

A. .doc

B. .exe

C. .jpg

D. .zip

Answer: A. .doc

Explanation: Macro viruses often target document file extensions like .doc.

16. What is the primary function of antivirus software?

A. Blocking network traffic

B. Monitoring system performance

C. Detecting and removing malware

D. Encrypting files

Answer: C. Detecting and removing malware

Explanation: Antivirus software detects and removes malicious software from systems.

17. How do attackers often propagate malware through networks?

A. By encrypting files

B. Through drive-by downloads

C. By sending phishing emails

D. By disabling firewalls

Answer: B. Through drive-by downloads

Explanation: Attackers spread malware by initiating automatic downloads from compromised websites.

18. What is a common purpose of utilizing malware by malicious actors?

A. Improving system performance

B. Gaining unauthorized access

C. Providing system security

D. Enhancing network speed

Answer: B. Gaining unauthorized access

Explanation: Malicious actors often use malware to gain unauthorized access to systems.

19. Which type of malware requires user interaction to execute?

A. Worm

B. Virus

C. Trojan

D. Backdoor

Answer: C. Trojan

Explanation: Trojans masquerade as legitimate software and require user interaction to execute.

20. What differentiates a backdoor from other malware?

A. It self-replicates

B. It requires user intervention

C. It provides unauthorized access

D. It remains dormant

Answer: C. It provides unauthorized access

Explanation: Backdoors provide unauthorized access to systems for malicious actors.

21. What is a key characteristic of a backdoor?

A. It self-replicates

B. It disguises itself as legitimate software

C. It provides unauthorized access

D. It spreads through network connections

Answer: C. It provides unauthorized access

Explanation: Backdoors allow unauthorized access to a system for malicious purposes.

22. How do worms differ from viruses?

A. Worms require user intervention to execute

B. Viruses spread independently without user interaction

C. Worms encrypt their code to avoid detection

D. Viruses primarily infect network connections

Answer: B. Viruses spread independently without user interaction

Explanation: Viruses can propagate independently without user intervention, whereas worms actively exploit vulnerabilities to spread.

23. During which stage of a virus' life does it execute malicious actions?

A. Dormant stage

B. Propagation stage

C. Triggering stage

D. Execution stage

Answer: D. Execution stage

Explanation: The execution stage involves the virus performing its intended actions, causing damage or replicating.

24. What distinguishes self-modifying viruses from other malware?

A. They replicate quickly

B. They encrypt their code to evade detection

C. They infect only specific file types

D. They require user interaction to spread

Answer: B. They encrypt their code to evade detection

Explanation: Self-modifying viruses alter their code or structure to avoid detection by antivirus software.

25. Which file extension is commonly targeted by macro viruses?

A. .doc

B. .exe

C. .jpg

D. .zip

Answer: A. .doc

Explanation: Macro viruses commonly infect document file extensions like .doc.

26. What is the primary function of antivirus software?

A. Blocking network traffic

B. Monitoring system performance

C. Detecting and removing malware

D. Encrypting files

Answer: C. Detecting and removing malware

Explanation: Antivirus software identifies and removes malicious software from systems.

27. How do attackers often propagate malware through networks?

A. By encrypting files

B. Through drive-by downloads

C. By sending phishing emails

D. By disabling firewalls

Answer: B. Through drive-by downloads

Explanation: Attackers spread malware through automatic downloads from compromised websites.

28. What is a common purpose of utilizing malware by malicious actors?

A. Improving system performance

B. Gaining unauthorized access

C. Providing system security

D. Enhancing network speed

Answer: B. Gaining unauthorized access

Explanation: Malicious actors often use malware to gain unauthorized access to systems.

29. Which type of malware requires user interaction to execute?

A. Worm

B. Virus

C. Trojan

D. Backdoor

Answer: C. Trojan

Explanation: Trojans require user interaction to execute and often masquerade as legitimate software.

30. What differentiates a backdoor from other malware?

A. It self-replicates

B. It requires user intervention

C. It provides unauthorized access

D. It remains dormant

Answer: C. It provides unauthorized access

Explanation: Backdoors enable unauthorized access to systems for malicious purposes.

Chapter 6: Sniffers and Social Engineering

Sniffers

Sniffers represent a category of tools designed to intercept and analyze network traffic, often without authorization. These tools are capable of capturing and inspecting data packets traversing a network, providing visibility into information exchanges between devices.

Switched Ethernet

In a switched Ethernet environment, traditional packet sniffing encounters limitations due to the switch's functionality. Unlike hubs, switches direct data packets to their intended destination ports, reducing the visibility of traffic for unauthorized parties attempting to capture information.

Types of Sniffing

Passive Sniffing

Passive sniffing involves monitoring network traffic without actively altering or interfering with it. This method allows the observer to gather information without triggering alarms or detection mechanisms.

Active Sniffing

Active sniffing engages in more intrusive techniques, involving modifications or injections into the network traffic for detailed analysis or control. This method poses a higher risk of being detected.

Sniffing, when used in a malicious context, can compromise sensitive data, including login credentials, financial information, or confidential communications. Mitigating these risks involves robust security measures, including encryption, network segmentation, and vigilant monitoring to detect unauthorized access.

Using social engineering, attackers exploit human psychology to manipulate individuals into divulging confidential information or performing actions that compromise security. This manipulation often relies on trust, authority, or urgency to deceive individuals.

Understanding the capabilities of sniffers, the limitations in switched Ethernet environments, and the varying types of sniffing methods is pivotal for implementing effective security protocols. Additionally, recognizing the dangers of social engineering emphasizes the importance of user education and stringent security policies to counter such deceptive tactics.

Protocols Vulnerable to Sniffing

Several protocols are vulnerable to packet sniffing due to their unencrypted nature, including:

HTTP (Hypertext Transfer Protocol): Transmitting data in plain text, making it susceptible to interception.

FTP (File Transfer Protocol): Insecurely transferring files, including credentials, without encryption.

Telnet: Sending commands and data in clear text, risking exposure to sniffing attacks.

SMTP (Simple Mail Transfer Protocol): Transmitting emails without encryption, potentially exposing content.

Electronic Surveillance

Electronic surveillance involves monitoring digital communications or activities for the purpose of gathering information. It encompasses various methods, including packet sniffing, to intercept and analyze data.

How to Detect Sniffing

Detecting sniffing activities involves several techniques:

Network Monitoring Tools: Using software like Wireshark to analyze network traffic for unusual patterns or unauthorized activities.

Traffic Analysis: Observing network performance changes or unexpected data transmissions.

Security Audits: Regularly assessing network logs and activities for anomalies or unauthorized access.

Wget

Wget is a command-line utility for retrieving content from web servers. While primarily used for legitimate purposes, it could potentially be misused by attackers for data retrieval.

Understanding vulnerable protocols susceptible to sniffing attacks, recognizing electronic surveillance methods, employing detection techniques like network monitoring tools and traffic analysis, and being aware of utilities like Wget help in identifying potential vulnerabilities and securing networks against unauthorized data interception.

Spearphishing Attack

A spearphishing attack is a targeted form of phishing where attackers tailor their deceptive messages to specific individuals or groups. It involves manipulating recipients into divulging sensitive information or performing actions that compromise security, often through emails or messages that appear legitimate.

Viewing Credentials

Gaining access to credentials involves various methods, including:

Phishing: Deceiving users into sharing login details through fake websites or emails.

Keylogging: Capturing keystrokes to obtain usernames and passwords.

Data Breaches: Acquiring login credentials from compromised databases.

Social Engineering

Social engineering manipulates human psychology to deceive individuals into divulging confidential information or performing actions that compromise security. It exploits trust, authority, or urgency to achieve its objectives.

Social Engineering Cycle

The social engineering cycle typically involves:

Reconnaissance: Gathering information about the target.

Creating Trust: Establishing credibility or trust with the target.

Exploiting Trust: Leveraging the established trust to deceive or manipulate.

Execution: Carrying out the intended objective, such as obtaining information or access.

Techniques

Social engineering employs various techniques, including:

Pretexting: Creating a fabricated scenario to extract information.

Phishing: Sending deceptive messages to obtain sensitive data.

Baiting: Offering something appealing to entice individuals to reveal information.

Tailgating: Gaining unauthorized physical access by following authorized personnel.

Computer-Based Social Engineering

Computer-based social engineering involves:

Phishing Emails: Sending deceptive emails to trick recipients into revealing credentials or downloading malware.

Fake Websites: Creating fraudulent websites to steal login details or financial information.

Malicious Software: Distributing malware through deceptive links or downloads.

Understanding the methods of spearphishing attacks, the manipulation involved in viewing credentials, the cycle and techniques of social engineering, and the diverse avenues used in computer-based social engineering is crucial for individuals and organizations to strengthen their defenses against such manipulative tactics.

It seems like "Shark" might refer to Wireshark, a popular network protocol analyzer. Here are some prevention recommendations, general defense measures, and countermeasures:

Prevention Recommendations for Wireshark (Shark) Attacks:

Encryption: Implement strong encryption protocols for sensitive data to prevent interception by packet analyzers like Wireshark.

Segmented Networks: Segregate critical network segments to limit access to sensitive data, reducing the impact of potential breaches.

Secure Configurations: Regularly update and secure systems, including firewalls and routers, to minimize vulnerabilities.

Traffic Monitoring: Deploy network monitoring tools to detect and respond to unusual traffic patterns or suspicious activities.

Access Control: Enforce strict access controls, including strong authentication measures and least privilege principles, to limit unauthorized access to network resources.

General Defense Measures:

Education and Awareness: Train users on recognizing phishing attempts, social engineering, and other tactics used in cyberattacks.

Multi-Factor Authentication (MFA): Implement MFA to add an extra layer of security, reducing the risk of unauthorized access even if credentials are compromised.

Regular Updates and Patching: Keep software, operating systems, and security tools up-to-date to address known vulnerabilities and strengthen defenses.

Incident Response Planning: Develop and practice incident response plans to swiftly respond to and mitigate the impact of security incidents.

Firewalls and Intrusion Prevention Systems (IPS): Employ firewalls and IPS to monitor and control incoming and outgoing traffic, preventing unauthorized access and detecting potential threats.

Countermeasures against Wireshark (Shark) Attacks:

Encryption Protocols: Implement end-to-end encryption for sensitive communications to prevent interception and deciphering of data packets.

Network Segmentation: Segment networks to restrict access, preventing attackers from easily accessing sensitive areas.

Packet Filtering: Employ packet-filtering techniques to discard packets that don't adhere to predefined security policies, minimizing the potential impact of sniffing attempts.

Monitoring and Intrusion Detection: Regularly monitor network traffic and use intrusion detection systems to identify anomalies or suspicious behavior indicative of a Wireshark-based attack.

Limiting Wireshark Access: Control access to Wireshark or similar packet analyzers, ensuring they are only accessible to authorized personnel for legitimate purposes.

Combining prevention strategies, general defense measures, and specific countermeasures tailored to mitigate the risks associated with Wireshark-based attacks can significantly enhance overall cybersecurity posture and protect against potential threats.

Practice Questions and Answers

1. Which type of tool is commonly used to capture and analyze network traffic?

A. Antivirus

B. Firewall

C. Sniffer

D. Encryption software

Answer: C. Sniffer

Explanation: A sniffer is a tool used to capture and analyze network traffic.

2. What is the primary vulnerability exploited by sniffers?

A. Weak passwords

B. Outdated software

C. Unencrypted data transmission

D. Network congestion

Answer: C. Unencrypted data transmission

Explanation: Sniffers exploit the vulnerability of unencrypted data transmissions, capturing sensitive information.

3. Which network protocol is vulnerable to packet sniffing due to its unencrypted nature?

A. HTTPS

B. FTP

C. SSH

D. VPN

Answer: B. FTP

Explanation: FTP transmits data in plain text, making it vulnerable to packet sniffing.

4. What makes switch-based networks less susceptible to sniffing attacks?

A. Encrypted data transmission

B. Increased network speed

C. Improved user authentication

D. Direct packet routing to intended ports

Answer: D. Direct packet routing to intended ports

Explanation: Switches direct packets only to their intended destination ports, reducing exposure to unauthorized sniffing.

5. Which type of sniffing involves monitoring network traffic without altering it?

A. Passive sniffing

B. Active sniffing

C. Malicious sniffing

D. Covert sniffing

Answer: A. Passive sniffing

Explanation: Passive sniffing involves monitoring network traffic without actively altering it.

6. What is a typical indication of a network undergoing active sniffing?

A. Decreased network latency

B. Increased data encryption

C. Unexplained data transmissions

D. Improved network throughput

Answer: C. Unexplained data transmissions

Explanation: Active sniffing can lead to unexplained data transmissions or unexpected traffic patterns.

Social Engineering:

7. What is the primary goal of social engineering attacks?

A. Encrypting data

B. Gaining unauthorized access

C. Increasing network bandwidth

D. Improving system performance

Answer: B. Gaining unauthorized access

Explanation: The primary goal of social engineering attacks is to gain unauthorized access or information.

8. Which technique relies on creating a fabricated scenario to extract sensitive information?

A. Phishing

B. Baiting

C. Pretexting

D. Tailgating

Answer: C. Pretexting

Explanation: Pretexting involves creating a false scenario to extract sensitive information from individuals.

9. What is the main psychological factor exploited in social engineering attacks?

A. Fear

B. Trust

C. Curiosity

D. Ambiguity

Answer: B. Trust

Explanation: Social engineering manipulates trust to deceive individuals into divulging confidential information.

10. Which social engineering technique involves enticing individuals with something appealing to extract information?

A. Phishing

B. Baiting

C. Pretexting

D. Tailgating

Answer: B. Baiting

Explanation: Baiting involves offering something appealing to entice individuals into revealing information.

11. How do sniffers intercept network traffic?

A. By encrypting data packets

B. By routing packets to specific ports

C. By capturing and analyzing packets

D. By increasing network bandwidth

Answer: C. By capturing and analyzing packets

Explanation: Sniffers intercept network traffic by capturing and analyzing data packets.

12. Which network protocol is susceptible to sniffing attacks due to transmitting data in plain text?

A. HTTPS

B. FTP

C. SSH

D. VPN

Answer: B. FTP

Explanation: FTP transmits data in plain text, making it vulnerable to sniffing attacks.

13. What security measure makes it harder for sniffers to intercept data on switched networks?

A. Packet encryption

B. Enhanced user authentication

C. Network segmentation

D. Increased bandwidth

Answer: C. Network segmentation

Explanation: Network segmentation reduces the exposure of data to unauthorized sniffing.

14. What differentiates passive from active sniffing?

A. Passive sniffing modifies network traffic

B. Active sniffing analyzes network traffic

C. Passive sniffing does not alter network traffic

D. Active sniffing encrypts captured packets

Answer: C. Passive sniffing does not alter network traffic

Explanation: Passive sniffing involves monitoring network traffic without actively altering it.

15. How does a switch differ from a hub concerning sniffing vulnerability?

A. Switches offer higher bandwidth

B. Hubs use encryption for data transmission

C. Switches route packets to specific ports

D. Hubs provide better user authentication

Answer: C. Switches route packets to specific ports

Explanation: Switches direct packets to their intended ports, reducing exposure to unauthorized sniffing.

Social Engineering:

16. What is the primary goal of social engineering attacks?

A. Enhancing system performance

B. Improving network security

C. Gaining unauthorized access

D. Increasing data encryption

Answer: C. Gaining unauthorized access

Explanation: Social engineering attacks aim to gain unauthorized access or information.

17. Which social engineering technique relies on creating urgency or panic to obtain sensitive information?

A. Pretexting

B. Phishing

C. Scareware

D. Tailgating

Answer: C. Scareware

Explanation: Scareware uses fear or urgency to manipulate individuals into divulging information.

18. What is the psychological factor exploited in baiting attacks?

A. Trust

B. Fear

C. Curiosity

D. Ambiguity

Answer: C. Curiosity

Explanation: Baiting preys on curiosity by offering something appealing to entice individuals.

19. Which technique involves creating a fictional scenario to extract sensitive information?

A. Tailgating

B. Baiting

C. Pretexting

D. Phishing

Answer: C. Pretexting

Explanation: Pretexting involves creating a fabricated scenario to extract sensitive information.

20. What is the primary tactic used in phishing attacks?

A. Creating trust

B. Exploiting fear

C. Manipulating curiosity

D. Deceptive emails or messages

Answer: D. Deceptive emails or messages

Explanation: Phishing primarily involves sending deceptive emails or messages to extract information.

21. What distinguishes passive sniffing from active sniffing?

A. Passive sniffing requires physical access to the network

B. Active sniffing captures data without altering it

C. Passive sniffing collects data without interacting with it

D. Active sniffing alters network traffic to gather data

Answer: C. Passive sniffing collects data without interacting with it

Explanation: Passive sniffing involves monitoring network traffic without actively altering it.

22. Which protocol is known for transmitting data in clear text, making it susceptible to sniffing attacks?

A. SMTP

B. HTTPS

C. SSH

D. VPN

Answer: A. SMTP

Explanation: SMTP (Simple Mail Transfer Protocol) transmits emails in plain text, susceptible to sniffing attacks.

23. In a switched network, why are sniffing attacks more challenging to execute?

A. Enhanced encryption

B. Increased bandwidth

C. Segmented network segments

D. Direct packet routing to specific ports

Answer: D. Direct packet routing to specific ports

Explanation: Switches direct packets to specific ports, limiting exposure to unauthorized sniffing.

24. What is a primary concern regarding unencrypted data in network transmissions?

A. Decreased network latency

B. Increased network throughput

C. Vulnerability to sniffing attacks

D. Improved data compression

Answer: C. Vulnerability to sniffing attacks

Explanation: Unencrypted data transmissions are vulnerable to interception by sniffing attacks.

25. Which sniffing technique involves altering network traffic for detailed analysis?

A. Passive sniffing

B. Active sniffing

C. Covert sniffing

D. Malicious sniffing

Answer: B. Active sniffing

Explanation: Active sniffing involves modifying or injecting data packets for detailed analysis.

Social Engineering:

26. What psychological factor does social engineering typically exploit?

A. Fear

B. Trust

C. Curiosity

D. Ambiguity

Answer: B. Trust

Explanation: Social engineering manipulates trust to deceive individuals into divulging information.

27. Which social engineering technique involves impersonating a legitimate entity to extract information?

A. Phishing

B. Pretexting

C. Tailgating

D. Baiting

Answer: B. Pretexting

Explanation: Pretexting involves creating a false scenario to extract sensitive information.

28. What's the primary objective of tailgating in social engineering?

A. Physical security breach

B. Gaining access to confidential information

C. Malware distribution

D. Encouraging data encryption

Answer: A. Physical security breach

Explanation: Tailgating involves gaining unauthorized physical access by following authorized personnel.

29. What social engineering technique uses fake enticing offers to obtain information?

A. Phishing

B. Baiting

C. Pretexting

D. Spoofing

Answer: B. Baiting

Explanation: Baiting offers something appealing to entice individuals into revealing information.

30. Which social engineering method typically involves deceptive emails or messages?

A. Phishing

B. Tailgating

C. Pretexting

D. Baiting

Answer: A. Phishing

Explanation: Phishing primarily involves sending deceptive emails or messages to extract information.

Chapter 7: Denial of Service

A Denial-of-Service attack aims to disrupt the availability of services or systems, rendering them inaccessible to legitimate users. This attack floods the target with an overwhelming volume of traffic or malicious requests, causing it to become unresponsive or unusable.

Types of DoS Attacks

Volume-Based Attacks: Overwhelm network bandwidth with a flood of traffic, like ICMP floods or UDP floods.

Protocol-Based Attacks: Exploit vulnerabilities in network protocols, such as SYN Floods targeting the TCP handshake process.

Application Layer Attacks: Target web applications or services to exhaust resources, like HTTP/HTTPS or DNS-based attacks.

Distributed Denial-of-Service (DDoS): Amplify attacks by utilizing multiple systems or networks, often controlled by botnets, to target a single system or network.

Zero-Day Attacks: Exploit vulnerabilities unknown to software vendors, making it challenging to defend against.

Spoofing Attacks: Mask the source of the attack by using falsified IP addresses, complicating mitigation efforts.

Understanding the diverse range of DoS attacks, including their methodologies and vectors, is crucial for implementing effective defensive strategies to mitigate the impact of such attacks on systems and networks.

Botnets

Botnets are networks of compromised computers (bots) controlled by attackers remotely. These bots are infected with malicious software, allowing attackers to control them collectively. Botnets are commonly used for various malicious activities, including DDoS attacks, spam dissemination, information theft, and more.

Conducting a DDoS Attack

Botnet Setup: The attacker infects numerous devices (computers, IoT devices) with malware, forming a botnet.

Command and Control (C&C): The attacker issues commands to the botnet from a centralized controller, instructing bots to launch an attack.

Attack Initiation: Bots flood the target server or network with massive traffic or requests, overwhelming its resources.

Impact: The target system becomes overloaded, resulting in service degradation or complete unavailability to legitimate users.

Distributed Denial of Service (DDoS) Attack

A Distributed Denial-of-Service attack is orchestrated using multiple sources (botnets or multiple computers) to flood a target with an excessive volume of data or requests. This coordinated attack overwhelms the target's resources, making its services inaccessible to legitimate users.

Characteristics of DDoS Attacks:

Large-Scale: Involves a massive volume of traffic generated from various sources.

Coordinated: Orchestrated by multiple attackers or compromised devices, amplifying the impact.

Multi-Layered: Targets various layers of the network stack, including application, transport, and network layers.

Stealthy: Can use various techniques like IP spoofing or encryption to evade detection and mitigation.

Resource Exhaustion: Aims to exhaust the target's computing resources, bandwidth, or network capacity.

DDoS attacks pose a significant threat due to their ability to disrupt services, causing financial losses, reputation damage, and downtime for businesses and organizations. Implementing robust security measures, network monitoring, and DDoS mitigation solutions is critical to defend against these attacks.

Attack Classes

1. Application Layer Attacks:

These target specific applications or services to overwhelm server resources. Examples include HTTP floods, Slowloris attacks, and DNS amplification.

2. Protocol-Based Attacks:

Exploit weaknesses in network protocols, like SYN Floods, aiming to exhaust server resources by consuming connection resources.

3. Volumetric Attacks:

Flood the target with high volumes of traffic, consuming available bandwidth, such as UDP floods or ICMP Echo requests.

4. Reflective/Amplification Attacks:

Utilize servers that respond to spoofed IP addresses with larger responses, amplifying the attack's impact (e.g., DNS amplification).

5. Zero-Day Exploits:

Exploit vulnerabilities in software or systems that vendors are unaware of, making mitigation more challenging.

Countermeasures

1. DDoS Mitigation Services:

Employ specialized services or hardware designed to detect and mitigate DDoS attacks in real-time.

2. Network Filtering and Firewalls:

Set up network filters or firewalls to block malicious traffic and prevent it from reaching the target.

3. Rate Limiting and Throttling:

Implement measures to control and limit the volume of incoming traffic to manageable levels.

4. Anomaly Detection Systems:

Use systems capable of identifying abnormal traffic patterns, allowing for rapid response to potential attacks.

5. Cloud-Based Protection:

Utilize cloud-based DDoS protection services that offer scalable resources to absorb and mitigate attacks.

Performing a DoS Attack

Performing a DoS attack requires various steps:

Preparation:

Identify potential targets and vulnerabilities. Set up the necessary tools or scripts to execute the attack.

Execution:

Launch the attack using a method that overwhelms the target with excessive traffic, requests, or resource depletion.

Observation:

Monitor the target's response to the attack, assessing its availability or degradation in service.

Cover Tracks:

Conceal traces of the attack by cleaning logs or erasing digital footprints to evade detection.

Performing a DoS attack is illegal and unethical. Engaging in such activities can result in severe legal consequences, including fines and imprisonment. It's crucial to use this knowledge responsibly and ethically, focusing on defensive strategies rather than launching attacks.

Practice Questions and Answers

1. What is the primary objective of a Denial of Service (DoS) attack?

A. Data theft

B. Resource depletion

C. Unauthorized access

D. Encryption

Answer: B. Resource depletion

Explanation: The primary goal of a DoS attack is to exhaust or overwhelm a target's resources, rendering it unavailable to legitimate users.

2. Which type of DoS attack overwhelms network bandwidth with a flood of traffic?

A. Protocol-based attack

B. Volumetric attack

C. Application layer attack

D. Zero-day attack

Answer: B. Volumetric attack

Explanation: Volumetric attacks flood the target with an excessive volume of traffic, consuming available bandwidth.

3. What distinguishes a DDoS attack from a DoS attack?

A. DDoS attacks involve multiple attackers

B. DoS attacks use encrypted traffic

C. DDoS attacks are slower

D. DoS attacks affect only application layers

Answer: A. DDoS attacks involve multiple attackers

Explanation: DDoS attacks involve multiple sources coordinating to attack a single target.

4. Which type of DoS attack exploits vulnerabilities in network protocols?

A. Application layer attack

B. Protocol-based attack

C. Volumetric attack

D. Reflective attack

Answer: B. Protocol-based attack

Explanation: Protocol-based attacks exploit weaknesses in network protocols to disrupt service.

5. What characterizes a reflective DDoS attack?

A. Attacks multiple layers simultaneously

B. Amplifies attack traffic using multiple sources

C. Redirects attack traffic through compromised servers

D. Targets specific applications or services

Answer: C. Redirects attack traffic through compromised servers

Explanation: Reflective attacks use servers to amplify and redirect attack traffic to the target.

6. How does a DDoS attack impact a targeted system?

A. Encrypts data

B. Increases system performance

C. Renders services unavailable

D. Enhances network security

Answer: C. Renders services unavailable

Explanation: A DDoS attack overwhelms the system, making services inaccessible to legitimate users.

7. What distinguishes zero-day attacks from other DoS attacks?

A. They exploit unknown vulnerabilities

B. They affect only application layers

C. They use encrypted traffic

D. They involve multiple attackers

Answer: A. They exploit unknown vulnerabilities

Explanation: Zero-day attacks leverage vulnerabilities unknown to vendors, making them harder to defend against.

8. Which layer of a network stack does an application layer attack typically target?

A. Network layer

B. Transport layer

C. Physical layer

D. Application layer

Answer: D. Application layer

Explanation: Application layer attacks target specific applications or services to disrupt service.

9. What's the primary goal of a volumetric DoS attack?

A. Targeting specific applications

B. Consuming network bandwidth

C. Exploiting vulnerabilities in protocols

D. Amplifying attack traffic

Answer: B. Consuming network bandwidth

Explanation: Volumetric attacks aim to overwhelm network bandwidth.

10. How does a protocol-based attack exploit network weaknesses?

A. By encrypting traffic

B. By flooding the network with requests

C. By overwhelming system resources

D. By exploiting flaws in network protocols

Answer: D. By exploiting flaws in network protocols

Explanation: Protocol-based attacks exploit weaknesses within network protocols to disrupt services.

11. What is the primary purpose of a Distributed Denial of Service (DDoS) attack?

A. Data encryption

B. Unauthorized access

C. Resource depletion

D. System performance improvement

Answer: C. Resource depletion

Explanation: The primary goal of a DDoS attack is to exhaust or overwhelm a target's resources.

12. Which attack type aims to consume a target's connection resources, hindering new connections?

A. Protocol-based attack

B. Volumetric attack

C. Application layer attack

D. SYN Flood attack

Answer: D. SYN Flood attack

Explanation: SYN Flood attacks flood a server with SYN requests, exhausting connection resources and preventing new connections.

13. What characterizes a reflective DoS attack?

A. Uses multiple attackers

B. Amplifies attack traffic through servers

C. Overwhelms bandwidth with traffic

D. Targets specific applications

Answer: B. Amplifies attack traffic through servers

Explanation: Reflective attacks leverage servers to amplify and redirect attack traffic to the target.

14. How does a DDoS attack differ from a DoS attack?

A. DDoS attacks use encrypted traffic

B. DoS attacks involve multiple sources

C. DDoS attacks target specific applications

D. DoS attacks are slower

Answer: B. DoS attacks involve multiple sources

Explanation: DDoS attacks involve multiple sources coordinating to attack a single target.

15. What is the main objective of a volumetric DoS attack?

A. Amplifying attack traffic

B. Disrupting specific applications

C. Overwhelming network bandwidth

D. Exploiting protocol weaknesses

Answer: C. Overwhelming network bandwidth

Explanation: Volumetric attacks aim to overwhelm network bandwidth, making services unavailable.

16. How do reflective DDoS attacks affect target systems?

A. Exhaust system resources

B. Redirect traffic through servers

C. Encrypt data packets

D. Slow down network speed

Answer: A. Exhaust system resources

Explanation: Reflective DDoS attacks aim to exhaust the target's resources, rendering services unavailable.

17. What differentiates zero-day attacks from other DoS attacks?

A. They target specific applications

B. They involve multiple attackers

C. They exploit unknown vulnerabilities

D. They encrypt attack traffic

Answer: C. They exploit unknown vulnerabilities

Explanation: Zero-day attacks leverage vulnerabilities unknown to vendors, making them harder to defend against.

18. Which layer of the network stack does an application layer attack typically target?

A. Physical layer

B. Transport layer

C. Network layer

D. Application layer

Answer: D. Application layer

Explanation: Application layer attacks specifically target applications or services.

19. What is the primary intention of a volumetric DoS attack?

A. Exploiting network vulnerabilities

B. Targeting specific applications

C. Overloading network bandwidth

D. Amplifying attack traffic

Answer: C. Overloading network bandwidth

Explanation: Volumetric attacks aim to overwhelm network bandwidth with an excessive volume of traffic.

20. How does a protocol-based attack disrupt network services?

A. By flooding the network with requests

B. By amplifying attack traffic

C. By targeting specific applications

D. By exploiting flaws in network protocols

Answer: D. By exploiting flaws in network protocols

Explanation: Protocol-based attacks exploit weaknesses within network protocols, disrupting network services.

21. What is the primary goal of a SYN Flood attack?

A. Consuming network bandwidth

B. Overloading server resources

C. Encrypting data packets

D. Redirecting attack traffic

Answer: B. Overloading server resources

Explanation: SYN Flood attacks exhaust server resources by flooding with SYN requests, hindering new connections.

22. Which attack type aims to exploit flaws in network protocols like TCP or UDP?

A. Protocol-based attack

B. Volumetric attack

C. Reflective attack

D. Zero-day attack

Answer: A. Protocol-based attack

Explanation: Protocol-based attacks exploit weaknesses in network protocols to disrupt services.

23. What defines a reflective DDoS attack?

A. It uses multiple attackers

B. It targets specific applications

C. It amplifies attack traffic through servers

D. It overwhelms network bandwidth

Answer: C. It amplifies attack traffic through servers

Explanation: Reflective attacks leverage servers to amplify and redirect attack traffic to the target.

24. What distinguishes a DoS attack from a DDoS attack?

A. DDoS attacks use encrypted traffic

B. DoS attacks target specific applications

C. DDoS attacks involve multiple sources

D. DoS attacks exploit zero-day vulnerabilities

Answer: C. DDoS attacks involve multiple sources

Explanation: DDoS attacks involve multiple sources coordinating to attack a single target.

25. What is the primary objective of a volumetric DoS attack?

A. Exploiting protocol weaknesses

B. Disrupting specific applications

C. Overwhelming network bandwidth

D. Redirecting attack traffic

Answer: C. Overwhelming network bandwidth

Explanation: Volumetric attacks aim to overwhelm network bandwidth, rendering services unavailable.

26. How do reflective DDoS attacks affect target systems?

A. Redirect traffic through servers

B. Slow down network speed

C. Encrypt data packets

D. Exhaust system resources

Answer: D. Exhaust system resources

Explanation: Reflective DDoS attacks aim to exhaust the target's resources, making services unavailable.

27. What makes zero-day attacks challenging to defend against?

A. They exploit well-known vulnerabilities

B. They use only encrypted traffic

C. They affect specific applications

D. They exploit unknown vulnerabilities

Answer: D. They exploit unknown vulnerabilities

Explanation: Zero-day attacks leverage vulnerabilities unknown to vendors, making them harder to defend against.

28. Which layer of the network stack does an application layer attack primarily target?

A. Network layer

B. Transport layer

C. Physical layer

D. Application layer

Answer: D. Application layer

Explanation: Application layer attacks specifically target applications or services.

29. What is the primary intention of a volumetric DoS attack?

A. Targeting specific applications

B. Overloading network bandwidth

C. Amplifying attack traffic

D. Exploiting network vulnerabilities

Answer: B. Overloading network bandwidth

Explanation: Volumetric attacks aim to overwhelm network bandwidth with excessive traffic.

30. How do protocol-based attacks disrupt network services?

A. By flooding the network with requests

B. By amplifying attack traffic

C. By targeting specific applications

D. By exploiting flaws in network protocols

Answer: D. By exploiting flaws in network protocols

Explanation: Protocol-based attacks exploit weaknesses within network protocols, disrupting network services.

Chapter 8: Session Hijacking

The TCP Stack

TCP (Transmission Control Protocol) is a fundamental communication protocol in computer networks. It operates within the Transport Layer of the TCP/IP model and ensures reliable, ordered, and error-checked delivery of data between devices. The TCP stack consists of three main components:

Sequence Numbers: Used to reassemble packets and maintain the order of data transmission.

Acknowledgment (ACK) Numbers: Confirm receipt of data packets.

Flags: Control bits in the TCP header that indicate the status of a connection, such as SYN, ACK, and FIN.

Three-Way Handshake

The three-way handshake is a procedure in establishing a TCP connection between a client and a server:

SYN (Synchronize): The client sends a SYN packet to the server to initiate a connection.

SYN-ACK (Synchronize-Acknowledge): The server responds with a SYN-ACK packet, acknowledging the request.

ACK (Acknowledge): The client sends an ACK packet to confirm receipt of the server's response, completing the connection setup.

Steps in Session Hijacking

Session Establishment: Monitor ongoing TCP connections to identify a target session.

Connection Spoofing: Mimic one of the communicating parties to intercept and manipulate the session.

Session Takeover: Inject forged packets to hijack the connection without either party's knowledge.

Exploitation: Use the hijacked session to execute unauthorized actions or eavesdrop on data.

Types of Session Hijacking

Packet Sniffing: Intercept and analyze packets to obtain session information and hijack connections.

Man-in-the-Middle (MITM): Position between the communicating parties to intercept and manipulate the session.

Session Sidejacking: Exploit insecure session management, often in web applications, to hijack user sessions.

Understanding the TCP stack, three-way handshake, steps involved in session hijacking, and the various types of session hijacking is crucial for implementing robust security measures to prevent such attacks.

Network-Layer and Application-Layer Hijacking

Network-Layer Hijacking

Definition: Network-layer hijacking involves manipulating or intercepting traffic at the IP or network layer. Attackers exploit vulnerabilities or weaknesses in routing protocols, DNS servers, or IP address allocation to redirect or manipulate traffic.

Characteristics:

Involves attacks like IP spoofing, where an attacker impersonates a trusted entity by falsifying the source IP address.

Manipulates routing tables or protocols (like BGP) to reroute traffic through unauthorized paths.

Can lead to traffic interception, data theft, or DoS attacks by redirecting legitimate traffic to malicious destinations.

Application-Layer Hijacking

Definition: Application-layer hijacking targets vulnerabilities within the application itself. Attackers exploit weaknesses in application code, sessions, or cookies to gain unauthorized access or control.

Characteristics:

Targets specific applications or services, exploiting vulnerabilities like session fixation or cookie-based attacks.

Involves manipulating session tokens, cookies, or credentials to impersonate legitimate users.

Can lead to unauthorized access, data theft, or manipulation of sensitive information within applications.

Countermeasures

Network-Layer Hijacking Countermeasures:

Route Authentication: Implement mechanisms like BGPsec to verify routing information authenticity.

Packet Filtering and ACLs: Use firewalls or Access Control Lists (ACLs) to restrict or filter incoming/outgoing traffic.

Strong Authentication: Employ strong authentication methods to prevent IP spoofing or unauthorized access.

Encryption: Implement IPsec or VPNs to encrypt traffic, preventing interception or manipulation.

Application-Layer Hijacking Countermeasures:

Web Application Firewalls (WAF): Deploy WAFs to filter and monitor HTTP/HTTPS traffic for suspicious activities or attacks.

Secure Coding Practices: Employ secure coding guidelines and perform regular code audits to identify and patch vulnerabilities.

Session Management: Implement secure session handling mechanisms, regularly regenerate session IDs, and use HTTPS to encrypt session data.

Multi-Factor Authentication (MFA): Enforce MFA to enhance user authentication security and prevent unauthorized access.

Browser Exploit

Definition: Browser exploits leverage vulnerabilities in web browsers to execute malicious code, gain unauthorized access, or control the browser remotely.

Characteristics:

Targets weaknesses in browser plugins, extensions, or unpatched software vulnerabilities.

Exploits JavaScript, HTML, or CSS to execute arbitrary code, leading to malware installation or data theft.

Can result in unauthorized access to sensitive information stored within the browser, like cookies or passwords.

Understanding and implementing a combination of network and application-level security measures, along with keeping software updated and patched, is crucial to mitigate network-layer hijacking, application-layer hijacking, and browser exploits.

Configured Settings

Definition: Configured settings refer to the specific configurations and settings implemented within systems, applications, or networks. These settings dictate how components behave, manage resources, or interact with users or other systems.

Characteristics:

System Configuration: Includes settings related to hardware, software, network, and user preferences.

Security Configurations: Encompass security settings like firewalls, access controls, encryption, and authentication methods.

Application Settings: Define how an application operates, including user permissions, data storage, and communication protocols.

Network Configurations: Specify network topology, addressing, routing, and traffic management settings.

Maintaining properly configured settings is essential to ensure system functionality, security, and efficiency. Misconfigured settings can lead to vulnerabilities, security breaches, or operational issues.

Spear Phish Attack

Definition: Spear phishing is a targeted phishing attack that focuses on a specific individual, organization, or group. Attackers personalize their messages to trick recipients into revealing sensitive information, clicking malicious links, or downloading malware.

Characteristics:

Personalization: Tailored messages using specific details or context relevant to the target.

Spoofed Identities: Pretends to be a trusted source or known entity to gain the victim's trust.

Social Engineering: Manipulates emotions, urgency, or authority to prompt immediate action.

Malicious Payload: Often includes malicious attachments, links, or requests for login credentials.

Spear phishing attacks exploit human vulnerabilities, relying on deception and manipulation. Effective security awareness training, email filtering, and multi-factor authentication can mitigate the risks associated with such attacks.

Exploiting the Victim Machine

Definition: Exploiting a victim machine involves leveraging vulnerabilities or weaknesses in a system to gain unauthorized access, control, or execute malicious actions.

Characteristics:

Vulnerability Identification: Identifies weaknesses, such as unpatched software, misconfigurations, or unsecured access points.

Attack Vector: Exploits vulnerabilities through malware, code execution, privilege escalation, or social engineering.

Compromise: Enables unauthorized access, data theft, or control over the victim's machine.

Payload Execution: Executes malicious code or instructions to achieve the attacker's objectives.

Proper patch management, strong access controls, regular security audits, and intrusion detection systems are essential to prevent and detect exploitation attempts on victim machines. Regular updates, security patches, and employee training can significantly reduce the risk of successful exploitation.

Practice Questions and Answers

1. What is the primary objective of session hijacking?

A. Data encryption

B. Resource depletion

C. Unauthorized access

D. System performance improvement

Answer: C. Unauthorized access

Explanation: Session hijacking aims to gain unauthorized access to a user's session or system.

2. What distinguishes session hijacking from other attacks?

A. It targets specific applications

B. It involves multiple attackers

C. It exploits weaknesses in session management

D. It uses encrypted traffic

Answer: C. It exploits weaknesses in session management

Explanation: Session hijacking exploits vulnerabilities in session handling to gain control or access.

3. How does session hijacking typically occur?

A. By exploiting weaknesses in routing protocols

B. By intercepting traffic at the transport layer

C. By manipulating session-related data

D. By encrypting session tokens

Answer: C. By manipulating session-related data

Explanation: Session hijacking involves manipulating session data to gain unauthorized access.

4. Which technique involves inserting fraudulent packets into an ongoing session to hijack it?

A. Packet filtering

B. Packet sniffing

C. Session fixation

D. Session takeover

Answer: D. Session takeover

Explanation: Session takeover involves inserting malicious packets to gain control over an ongoing session.

5. What is the primary goal of a session hijacking attack?

A. Data encryption

B. Resource depletion

C. Unauthorized access

D. System performance improvement

Answer: C. Unauthorized access

Explanation: Session hijacking aims to gain unauthorized access to a user's session or system.

6. Which attack method involves intercepting and manipulating traffic between two communicating parties?

A. Session fixation

B. Man-in-the-Middle (MITM)

C. Session sidejacking

D. Cross-Site Scripting (XSS)

Answer: B. Man-in-the-Middle (MITM)

Explanation: MITM attacks involve intercepting and manipulating traffic between parties, including session data.

7. What does a session hijacking attacker aim to achieve?

A. Legitimate access

B. Data integrity

C. Unauthorized access

D. System optimization

Answer: C. Unauthorized access

Explanation: Session hijacking seeks unauthorized access to systems or sessions.

8. What is the primary method of preventing session hijacking attacks?

A. Regular data backups

B. Strong encryption

C. Secure session management

D. Intrusion Detection Systems (IDS)

Answer: C. Secure session management

Explanation: Secure session management helps prevent session hijacking attacks.

9. How can an attacker manipulate sessions to gain unauthorized access?

A. By encrypting session data

B. By injecting malicious code into sessions

C. By compressing session cookies

D. By increasing session timeout duration

Answer: B. By injecting malicious code into sessions

Explanation: Attackers can inject malicious code into sessions to gain unauthorized access.

10. What is the primary concern of session hijacking?

A. Data encryption

B. Unauthorized access

C. Resource depletion

D. System performance

Answer: B. Unauthorized access

Explanation: Session hijacking's primary concern is gaining unauthorized access to sessions or systems.

11. What differentiates session hijacking from other cyber attacks?

A. It involves code injection

B. It exploits weaknesses in session management

C. It relies on network packet analysis

D. It targets hardware vulnerabilities

Answer: B. It exploits weaknesses in session management

Explanation: Session hijacking exploits flaws in how sessions are managed to gain unauthorized access.

12. Which method involves an attacker predicting or injecting a valid session identifier to gain control?

A. Session sniffing

B. Session fixation

C. Man-in-the-Middle (MITM)

D. Cross-Site Scripting (XSS)

Answer: B. Session fixation

Explanation: Session fixation involves an attacker setting or predicting a valid session ID to hijack a session.

13. What's the primary objective of an attacker in session hijacking?

A. Resource depletion

B. Unauthorized access

C. Data encryption

D. System performance improvement

Answer: B. Unauthorized access

Explanation: Attackers aim to gain unauthorized access to systems or sessions through session hijacking.

14. How can an attacker perpetrate session hijacking?

A. By encrypting session tokens

B. By impersonating legitimate users

C. By manipulating session data

D. By installing antivirus software

Answer: C. By manipulating session data

Explanation: Attackers manipulate session data to gain control over sessions.

15. What makes session hijacking a security concern?

A. Loss of system performance

B. Unauthorized access

C. Improved data encryption

D. Resource optimization

Answer: B. Unauthorized access

Explanation: Session hijacking poses a risk by granting unauthorized access to systems or sessions.

16. What is the primary vulnerability exploited in session hijacking attacks?

A. Weak encryption algorithms

B. Poor session management

C. Inadequate antivirus protection

D. Insufficient network bandwidth

Answer: B. Poor session management

Explanation: Session hijacking exploits weaknesses in how sessions are managed by systems or applications.

17. Which attack technique allows an attacker to eavesdrop on an ongoing session?

A. Cross-Site Scripting (XSS)

B. Session sniffing

C. Man-in-the-Middle (MITM)

D. SQL Injection

Answer: C. Man-in-the-Middle (MITM)

Explanation: MITM attacks intercept and manipulate traffic between parties, including session data.

18. What is the goal of session hijacking?

A. Data encryption

B. Unauthorized access

C. System optimization

D. Resource depletion

Answer: B. Unauthorized access

Explanation: Session hijacking seeks unauthorized access to systems or sessions.

19. How can organizations mitigate session hijacking risks?

A. Implementing weak encryption

B. Utilizing unsecured networks

C. Regularly updating security patches

D. Neglecting session timeouts

Answer: C. Regularly updating security patches

Explanation: Regularly updating security patches helps prevent vulnerabilities that attackers exploit in session hijacking.

20. Which action can enhance security against session hijacking?

A. Implementing strong session management

B. Sharing session cookies

C. Avoiding encryption of session data

D. Using default passwords

Answer: A. Implementing strong session management

Explanation: Strong session management helps prevent session hijacking by implementing robust security measures.

21. How does session hijacking differ from typical cyber attacks?

A. It involves server compromise

B. It exploits session management vulnerabilities

C. It focuses on hardware vulnerabilities

D. It uses strong encryption algorithms

Answer: B. It exploits session management vulnerabilities

Explanation: Session hijacking relies on weaknesses in how sessions are handled to gain unauthorized access.

22. What makes session hijacking a security risk?

A. Increased system performance

B. Unauthorized access

C. Enhanced data encryption

D. Improved network bandwidth

Answer: B. Unauthorized access

Explanation: Session hijacking poses a risk by granting unauthorized access to systems or sessions.

23. Which method allows an attacker to take control of an ongoing session?

A. Session encryption

B. Session sniffing

C. Session timeout

D. Session encryption

Answer: B. Session sniffing

Explanation: Session sniffing involves intercepting and analyzing traffic to gain control over an ongoing session.

24. What is the primary goal of an attacker using session hijacking?

A. System optimization

B. Data encryption

C. Resource depletion

D. Unauthorized access

Answer: D. Unauthorized access

Explanation: Attackers aim to gain unauthorized access to systems or sessions through session hijacking.

25. What vulnerability is commonly exploited in session hijacking attacks?

A. Weak password protection

B. Poor firewall configurations

C. Insecure data encryption

D. Flaws in session management

Answer: D. Flaws in session management

Explanation: Session hijacking exploits weaknesses in how sessions are managed by systems or applications.

26. How can an attacker perpetrate session hijacking?

A. By encrypting session tokens

B. By impersonating legitimate users

C. By manipulating session data

D. By installing antivirus software

Answer: C. By manipulating session data

Explanation: Attackers manipulate session data to gain control over sessions.

27. What is the primary concern of session hijacking?

A. Loss of system performance

B. Unauthorized access

C. Improved data encryption

D. Resource optimization

Answer: B. Unauthorized access

Explanation: Session hijacking poses a risk by granting unauthorized access to systems or sessions.

28. What is the primary vulnerability exploited in session hijacking attacks?

A. Weak encryption algorithms

B. Poor session management

C. Inadequate antivirus protection

D. Insufficient network bandwidth

Answer: B. Poor session management

Explanation: Session hijacking exploits weaknesses in how sessions are managed by systems or applications.

29. Which attack technique allows an attacker to eavesdrop on an ongoing session?

A. Cross-Site Scripting (XSS)

B. Session sniffing

C. Man-in-the-Middle (MITM)

D. SQL Injection

Answer: C. Man-in-the-Middle (MITM)

Explanation: MITM attacks intercept and manipulate traffic between parties, including session data.

30. What is the goal of session hijacking?

A. Data encryption

B. Unauthorized access

C. System optimization

D. Resource depletion

Answer: B. Unauthorized access

Explanation: Session hijacking seeks unauthorized access to systems or sessions.

Chapter 9: Hacking Webservers

Web servers often have vulnerabilities that hackers can exploit to gain unauthorized access or disrupt services. These vulnerabilities might include outdated software, misconfigurations, weak passwords, or unpatched security flaws.

Characteristics:

Outdated Software: Running older versions of server software that have known vulnerabilities.

Misconfigurations: Improperly configured settings or permissions, such as directory browsing enabled or default credentials unchanged.

Inadequate Security Measures: Weak password policies, lack of encryption, or absence of security updates.

Types of Risks

1. Unauthorized Access: Hackers can gain access to confidential files, databases, or configurations, leading to data breaches or system compromise.

2. Denial of Service (DoS): Attackers overload web servers with excessive traffic, rendering services inaccessible to legitimate users.

3. Defacement: Hackers alter the appearance or content of web pages, often to spread a message or disrupt operations.

4. Data Leakage: Leaking sensitive information due to insecure configurations or unencrypted data transmission.

Web Server Attacks

1. SQL Injection (SQLi): Exploiting SQL vulnerabilities to manipulate or retrieve data from databases.

2. Cross-Site Scripting (XSS): Injecting malicious scripts into web pages, often targeting users to execute arbitrary code.

3. Remote Code Execution (RCE): Exploiting vulnerabilities to execute arbitrary code on the server remotely.

4. Directory Traversal: Accessing restricted directories or files by manipulating URL inputs.

5. Brute Force Attacks: Repeatedly attempting to log in using various password combinations to gain access.

Understanding these vulnerabilities and attack methods is crucial to implementing effective security measures and ensuring the safety of web servers and the data they host.

IIS Components

Internet Information Services (IIS) is a web server software developed by Microsoft, primarily used to host websites and web applications on Windows servers. Key components of IIS include:

HTTP.sys: The kernel-mode driver that handles HTTP requests and manages low-level communication between the server and clients.

IIS Admin Service: Manages server configuration and performs administrative tasks for IIS.

WWW Service: Responsible for handling HTTP requests, processing ASP.NET applications, and serving web pages.

FTP Service: Facilitates file transfer functionalities, allowing users to upload/download files using the FTP protocol.

SMTP Service: Handles email delivery using the Simple Mail Transfer Protocol, often used in applications for sending emails.

IIS Logs

IIS generates logs that contain valuable information about server activities, requests, errors, and user interactions. These logs include:

HTTP Logs: Record information about each HTTP request, including client IP addresses, requested URLs, response status codes, and server processing time.

FTP Logs: Store details of FTP transactions, such as file uploads/downloads, user login attempts, and commands executed.

Event Logs: Contain system-level events and errors, including application crashes, service failures, or security-related incidents.

Web Server Security

Web server security involves implementing measures to protect servers and the data they host from various threats, ensuring confidentiality, integrity, and availability. Key security practices include:

Regular Updates: Applying security patches and updates to the operating system, server software, and applications to address vulnerabilities.

Access Control: Implementing strict access controls, using strong passwords, and limiting privileges to authorized personnel.

Encryption: Enabling SSL/TLS encryption to secure data transmitted between clients and the server, especially for sensitive information like login credentials.

Firewalls and Intrusion Detection Systems (IDS/IPS): Deploying firewalls to filter incoming/outgoing traffic and IDS/IPS to detect and prevent suspicious activities.

Backup and Recovery: Regularly backing up server data and implementing disaster recovery plans to mitigate potential data loss or server compromise.

Web Server Security Checklist

Update Software: Keep operating systems, server software, and applications up to date with the latest security patches.

Secure Configurations: Harden server configurations, disable unnecessary services, and use strong passwords.

Access Controls: Implement proper access controls and user authentication mechanisms.

Encryption: Enable SSL/TLS encryption and secure sensitive data transmission.

Monitoring and Logging: Regularly review server logs for suspicious activities and implement monitoring solutions.

Backup and Recovery: Perform regular backups and ensure reliable disaster recovery plans.

Following a comprehensive security checklist helps in maintaining the integrity and security of web servers, safeguarding against potential threats and vulnerabilities.

Apache Web Server Security Checklist

For securing an Apache web server, here's a comprehensive checklist:

Update Apache: Ensure Apache is running the latest stable version with security patches applied.

Secure Configuration: Adjust configuration files (httpd.conf, ssl.conf) to minimize information disclosure and limit server signature.

Access Controls: Implement IP-based access controls, configure firewalls, and use .htaccess files for directory restrictions.

SSL/TLS Encryption: Enable SSL/TLS encryption for secure data transmission (HTTPS), using strong ciphers and certificates.

Mod_Security: Deploy Mod_Security to mitigate common web application vulnerabilities like SQL Injection and XSS attacks.

File Permissions: Set appropriate file and directory permissions to limit access to sensitive data.

Regular Backups: Perform regular backups of website data and configurations.

Error Handling: Configure error pages to avoid exposing server details and prevent information leakage.

Logging and Monitoring: Enable logging and regularly monitor logs for suspicious activities or potential attacks.

Security Modules: Utilize security modules like mod_evasive to mitigate DoS attacks and mod_security for web application security.

Using Armitage to Attack the Network

Armitage is a graphical cyber attack management tool used for penetration testing and network exploitation. It streamlines the process of launching attacks against a network by providing an intuitive interface for Metasploit.

Steps to use Armitage:

Launch Armitage: Open Armitage after installing it on your system.

Connect to Metasploit: Armitage connects to the Metasploit Framework for performing attacks.

Host Discovery: Use Armitage for network discovery to identify live hosts and services running on the network.

Vulnerability Scanning: Perform vulnerability scans to identify weaknesses in discovered hosts.

Exploitation: Select a target and choose exploits or attacks from Metasploit's database to exploit vulnerabilities.

Post-Exploitation: Gain control of exploited systems and perform post-exploitation activities like privilege escalation or data exfiltration.

Using Armitage

Launching Attacks: Use Armitage's interface to select targets, choose attacks, and launch exploits against vulnerable systems.

Exploit Database: Armitage integrates with Metasploit's extensive exploit database, providing a wide range of attack vectors.

Visual Representation: Armitage offers a graphical representation of the attack surface, making it user-friendly and aiding in attack planning.

Post-Exploitation Tools: It includes post-exploitation tools for maintaining access, gathering information, and pivoting through networks.

When using Armitage or any other penetration testing tool, ensure it's done ethically and legally, preferably in a controlled environment with proper authorization. Unauthorized use can lead to legal consequences.

Practice Question and Answers

1. What is the primary objective of hacking a web server?

A. Gain unauthorized access

B. Enhance server performance

C. Improve data encryption

D. Strengthen firewall configurations

Answer: A. Gain unauthorized access

Explanation: Hacking a web server often aims to gain unauthorized access to data or control over the server.

2. What vulnerability might be exploited in a web server to gain access to sensitive files?

A. SQL Injection

B. Cross-Site Scripting (XSS)

C. Directory Traversal

D. Brute Force Attack

Answer: C. Directory Traversal

Explanation: Directory Traversal attacks exploit a vulnerability to access restricted files or directories on a server.

3. What is the goal of a Denial-of-Service (DoS) attack on a web server?

A. Unauthorized access

B. Data encryption

C. Server performance disruption

D. System optimization

Answer: C. Server performance disruption

Explanation: DoS attacks aim to disrupt server performance, making services unavailable to legitimate users.

4. Which attack type manipulates user input to execute malicious code on a web server?

A. SQL Injection

B. Cross-Site Scripting (XSS)

C. Brute Force Attack

D. Remote Code Execution (RCE)

Answer: B. Cross-Site Scripting (XSS)

Explanation: XSS attacks inject malicious scripts into web pages to execute code on users' browsers or servers.

5. What is the primary risk associated with an SQL Injection attack on a web server?

A. Unauthorized access

B. Data encryption

C. Directory traversal

D. Server performance disruption

Answer: A. Unauthorized access

Explanation: SQL Injection attacks aim to gain unauthorized access to databases and sensitive information.

6. How does a Brute Force Attack typically target a web server?

A. By exploiting misconfigured settings

B. By intercepting network traffic

C. By guessing passwords or credentials

D. By injecting malicious code

Answer: C. By guessing passwords or credentials

Explanation: Brute Force Attacks attempt to guess passwords or credentials to gain access.

7. What does a DoS attack on a web server seek to achieve?

A. Unauthorized access

B. Enhanced encryption

C. Server performance disruption

D. System optimization

Answer: C. Server performance disruption

Explanation: DoS attacks aim to disrupt server performance, rendering services inaccessible.

8. What vulnerability might an attacker exploit to execute arbitrary code on a web server?

A. SQL Injection

B. Directory Traversal

C. Cross-Site Scripting (XSS)

D. Remote Code Execution (RCE)

Answer: D. Remote Code Execution (RCE)

Explanation: RCE vulnerabilities allow attackers to execute arbitrary code on the server.

9. What is the primary concern of a Directory Traversal attack on a web server?

A. Unauthorized access

B. Data encryption

C. Server performance disruption

D. Brute Force Attack

Answer: A. Unauthorized access

Explanation: Directory Traversal attacks aim to access restricted files or directories.

10. How does Cross-Site Scripting (XSS) affect web servers?

A. Manipulates server settings

B. Executes code on the user's browser

C. Disrupts server performance

D. Increases data encryption

Answer: B. Executes code on the user's browser

Explanation: XSS attacks inject and execute malicious code on users' browsers rather than the server.

Hacking Web Servers:

11. What is the primary objective of a SQL Injection attack on a web server?

A. Remote Code Execution

B. Server Performance Disruption

C. Data Leakage

D. Directory Traversal

Answer: C. Data Leakage

Explanation: SQL Injection attacks aim to extract or leak data from databases accessed by the web server.

12. How does a Brute Force Attack typically affect a web server?

A. It exploits vulnerabilities in the server's configuration

B. It intercepts network traffic

C. It attempts to guess passwords or credentials

D. It executes arbitrary code on the server

Answer: C. It attempts to guess passwords or credentials

Explanation: Brute Force Attacks try various password combinations to gain unauthorized access.

13. What vulnerability might be exploited in a web server to execute commands remotely?

A. Directory Traversal

B. SQL Injection

C. Remote Code Execution (RCE)

D. Cross-Site Scripting (XSS)

Answer: C. Remote Code Execution (RCE)

Explanation: RCE vulnerabilities allow attackers to execute commands on the server remotely.

14. What risk does a DoS attack pose to a web server?

A. Unauthorized access

B. Data encryption

C. Server performance disruption

D. System optimization

Answer: C. Server performance disruption

Explanation: DoS attacks disrupt server performance by overwhelming it with excessive traffic.

15. How does a Directory Traversal attack impact a web server?

A. It disrupts server performance

B. It increases data encryption

C. It grants unauthorized access to restricted files or directories

D. It executes code on the user's browser

Answer: C. It grants unauthorized access to restricted files or directories

Explanation: Directory Traversal attacks aim to access files or directories beyond the server's intended scope.

16. What is the primary concern of an SQL Injection attack on a web server?

A. Data Leakage

B. Server Performance Disruption

C. Directory Traversal

D. Remote Code Execution

Answer: A. Data Leakage

Explanation: SQL Injection attacks target databases to extract or leak sensitive data.

17. How does a Cross-Site Scripting (XSS) attack impact users interacting with a web server?

A. It disrupts server performance

B. It leaks data from the server

C. It executes code on the user's browser

D. It grants access to restricted directories

Answer: C. It executes code on the user's browser

Explanation: XSS attacks execute malicious code on users' browsers, compromising their session.

18. What does a Brute Force Attack aim to achieve on a web server?

A. Remote Code Execution

B. Server Performance Optimization

C. Guessing passwords or credentials

D. Exploiting server misconfigurations

Answer: C. Guessing passwords or credentials

Explanation: Brute Force Attacks attempt to guess login credentials to gain access.

19. What vulnerability might an attacker exploit in a web server to modify URL parameters and access restricted files?

A. Directory Traversal

B. SQL Injection

C. Remote Code Execution (RCE)

D. Cross-Site Scripting (XSS)

Answer: A. Directory Traversal

Explanation: Directory Traversal exploits URL parameters to access files or directories beyond their intended scope.

20. What is the primary goal of a Remote Code Execution (RCE) attack on a web server?

A. Data Leakage

B. Server Performance Disruption

C. Executing arbitrary code on the server

D. Gaining unauthorized access

Answer: C. Executing arbitrary code on the server

Explanation: RCE attacks aim to execute arbitrary code on the server, often leading to complete compromise.

21. How does a Cross-Site Scripting (XSS) attack typically affect a web server?

A. It disrupts server performance

B. It injects and executes code on users' browsers

C. It guesses passwords or credentials

D. It exploits misconfigured server settings

Answer: B. It injects and executes code on users' browsers

Explanation: XSS attacks inject malicious scripts into web pages, affecting users' browsers rather than the server directly.

22. What risk does a Directory Traversal attack pose to a web server?

A. Unauthorized access to restricted files or directories

B. Increased data encryption

C. Server performance disruption

D. Executing code on the user's browser

Answer: A. Unauthorized access to restricted files or directories

Explanation: Directory Traversal attacks aim to bypass access controls and access files or directories beyond the server's intended scope.

23. What vulnerability might an attacker exploit to gain unauthorized access to databases connected to a web server?

A. Directory Traversal

B. SQL Injection

C. Remote Code Execution (RCE)

D. Brute Force Attack

Answer: B. SQL Injection

Explanation: SQL Injection attacks manipulate SQL queries to gain unauthorized access to databases.

24. How does a Brute Force Attack affect a web server?

A. It exploits vulnerabilities in server configurations

B. It disrupts server performance by overwhelming it with traffic

C. It attempts to guess passwords or credentials

D. It executes arbitrary code on the server

Answer: C. It attempts to guess passwords or credentials

Explanation: Brute Force Attacks try various password combinations to gain unauthorized access.

25. What is the primary concern of an SQL Injection attack on a web server?

A. Data Leakage

B. Server Performance Disruption

C. Directory Traversal

D. Remote Code Execution

Answer: A. Data Leakage

Explanation: SQL Injection attacks aim to extract or leak sensitive data from databases.

26. How does a DoS attack impact a web server?

A. Unauthorized access to sensitive files

B. Increased data encryption

C. Server performance disruption by overwhelming it with traffic

D. Executing code on the user's browser

Answer: C. Server performance disruption by overwhelming it with traffic

Explanation: DoS attacks aim to render services unavailable by overloading the server with excessive traffic.

27. What risk does a Remote Code Execution (RCE) vulnerability pose to a web server?

A. Unauthorized access to directories

B. Increased data encryption

C. Executing arbitrary code on the server

D. Server performance optimization

Answer: C. Executing arbitrary code on the server

Explanation: RCE vulnerabilities allow attackers to execute arbitrary code on the server, potentially leading to complete compromise.

28. How does a Cross-Site Scripting (XSS) attack affect users interacting with a web server?

A. Unauthorized access to directories

B. Increased data encryption

C. Injecting and executing code on users' browsers

D. Server performance disruption

Answer: C. Injecting and executing code on users' browsers

Explanation: XSS attacks execute malicious code on users' browsers, compromising their session or stealing information.

29. What vulnerability might an attacker exploit to access sensitive files by manipulating URL inputs?

A. SQL Injection

B. Directory Traversal

C. Remote Code Execution (RCE)

D. Brute Force Attack

Answer: B. Directory Traversal

Explanation: Directory Traversal exploits URL inputs to access files or directories beyond the intended scope.

30. How does a SQL Injection attack impact databases connected to a web server?

A. Unauthorized access to directories

B. Increased data encryption

C. Data leakage or unauthorized access to sensitive information

D. Executing code on the user's browser

Answer: C. Data leakage or unauthorized access to sensitive information

Explanation: SQL Injection attacks manipulate SQL queries, gaining unauthorized access or leaking sensitive data from connected databases.

Chapter 10: Hacking Web Applications

Web Application Attacks

Definition: Web application attacks target vulnerabilities in web-based software, aiming to exploit flaws in input validation, authentication mechanisms, or server configurations. Some common attacks include SQL Injection, Cross-Site Scripting (XSS), Cross-Site Request Forgery (CSRF), and more.

Cross-Site Scripting (XSS) Attack

Explanation: XSS attacks inject malicious scripts into web pages viewed by other users. This attack takes advantage of web applications that accept untrusted data and dynamically include it in the web page content, allowing the attacker to execute arbitrary scripts in the victim's browser.

Countermeasures for XSS Attacks

Input Validation: Implement strict input validation to filter and sanitize user inputs, preventing the insertion of malicious scripts.

Output Encoding: Encode user-generated content before rendering it on web pages to neutralize potential scripts, using functions like HTML escaping.

Content Security Policy (CSP): Implement CSP to define the allowed sources for content, reducing the impact of XSS attacks by limiting the execution of scripts.

HTTPOnly Cookies: Utilize HTTPOnly cookies to prevent JavaScript from accessing sensitive session cookies, reducing the risk of session hijacking.

Regular Security Audits: Conduct regular security audits and code reviews to identify and mitigate potential XSS vulnerabilities.

Additional Notes:

XSS Impact: XSS attacks can result in session hijacking, cookie theft, data manipulation, and phishing attacks against users.

Stored XSS vs. Reflected XSS: Stored XSS involves injecting scripts that persist in the application's database or storage, affecting multiple users, while Reflected XSS involves the immediate execution of injected scripts via URLs or input fields, affecting individual users.

Understanding these attacks and implementing effective countermeasures is crucial to safeguarding web applications against potential vulnerabilities and ensuring user data security.

SQL Injection

Definition: SQL Injection is a type of attack that exploits vulnerabilities in a web application's database layer by inserting malicious SQL queries into input fields. It allows attackers to manipulate or access a database, potentially extracting sensitive information or performing unauthorized actions.

Countermeasures:

Input Sanitization: Validate and sanitize user inputs to prevent the execution of injected SQL commands.

Use Prepared Statements or Parameterized Queries: Utilize prepared statements or parameterized queries to avoid direct concatenation of SQL queries with user inputs.

Least Privilege: Assign minimal database privileges to application users, limiting the scope of potential damage if an SQL Injection occurs.

Regular Security Audits: Conduct regular code reviews and security assessments to detect and mitigate vulnerabilities.

Cookie/Session Poisoning

Definition: Cookie or session poisoning involves manipulating or tampering with cookies or session data to gain unauthorized access or perform malicious actions. Attackers can modify cookie values or session variables to impersonate users or escalate privileges.

Countermeasures:

Secure Cookies: Use secure flags, HTTPOnly flags, and SameSite attributes to enhance cookie security.

Session Token Rotation: Implement session token rotation to change session IDs after certain intervals, reducing the window of opportunity for attackers.

Encrypt Sensitive Data: Encrypt sensitive information stored in cookies or sessions to prevent tampering.

Session Timeout: Set reasonable session timeout periods to minimize the impact of stolen or manipulated sessions.

Parameter/Form Tampering

Definition: Parameter or form tampering involves modifying hidden fields or parameters in web forms to alter application behavior or gain unauthorized access. Attackers manipulate input fields to change form values, alter URLs, or manipulate HTTP requests.

Countermeasures:

Server-Side Validation: Implement strong server-side validation for all input fields, ensuring data integrity.

Use of Integrity Checks: Apply digital signatures or checksums to form parameters to detect tampering.

Encrypted Connections: Utilize HTTPS to encrypt data transmitted between the client and server, reducing the risk of interception and modification.

Hidden Field Encryption: Encrypt sensitive hidden fields or parameters to prevent tampering.

Buffer Overflow

Definition: Buffer Overflow occurs when a program writes data beyond the bounds of an allocated memory buffer, leading to the execution of malicious code or crashing the application. Attackers exploit this vulnerability to inject and execute arbitrary code.

Countermeasures:

Input Validation: Validate and sanitize user inputs to prevent excessively long or malformed data that can trigger buffer overflows.

Memory Protection Mechanisms: Use memory protection mechanisms such as Data Execution Prevention (DEP) or Address Space Layout Randomization (ASLR) to mitigate buffer overflow risks.

Secure Coding Practices: Follow secure coding guidelines, use safer string manipulation functions, and perform bounds checking to prevent buffer overflow vulnerabilities.

Regular Patching: Keep systems and software updated with the latest security patches to address known buffer overflow vulnerabilities.

Implementing these countermeasures helps mitigate the risks associated with these attacks, strengthening the security posture of web applications and systems.

Error Message Interception

Definition: Error message interception involves exploiting error messages generated by applications or systems to gather information useful for launching further attacks. Attackers analyze error messages to identify vulnerabilities, system configurations, or sensitive information inadvertently disclosed.

Countermeasures:

Custom Error Handling: Implement custom error messages to provide minimal information to users without disclosing sensitive details.

Logging and Monitoring: Log errors on the server-side without revealing critical information and monitor logs for suspicious activities.

User-Friendly Error Messages: Provide generic error messages to users without revealing system details or internal configurations.

Regular Error Message Review: Periodically review error messages to ensure they do not disclose sensitive information.

Other Attacks

Definition: "Other Attacks" is a broad category covering various cyber attacks beyond the previously mentioned ones. This includes attacks such as Man-in-the-Middle (MITM), DNS Spoofing, Clickjacking, Session Fixation, and more.

Countermeasures:

Defense-in-Depth: Implement multiple layers of security controls to protect against various attack vectors.

Security Awareness Training: Educate users and developers about different attack methods and how to recognize and respond to them.

Regular Security Assessments: Conduct regular security assessments, penetration testing, and audits to identify vulnerabilities and weaknesses.

Network Segmentation: Segment networks to isolate critical systems and reduce the impact of successful attacks.

Using Nmap

Nmap (Network Mapper) is a widely used open-source tool for network discovery and security auditing. It helps in mapping network topology, identifying open ports, services, and other attributes of networked systems.

Usage: Nmap commands typically include:

nmap -sn [Target]: Performs a ping scan to discover live hosts.

nmap -sS [Target]: Initiates a SYN stealth scan to identify open ports.

nmap -A [Target]: Conducts an aggressive scan, providing detailed information about the target.

nmap -p [Ports] [Target]: Scans specific ports on a target.

Using ncat

Ncat is a networking utility similar to the nc (netcat) command, providing functionality for reading from and writing to network connections. It can be used for port scanning, banner grabbing, transferring files, or creating backdoors.

Usage: Common ncat commands include:

ncat [Host] [Port]: Initiates a connection to a specified host and port.

ncat -l [Port]: Listens for incoming connections on a specified port.

ncat -e [Program] [Host] [Port]: Executes a specified program upon connection.

Establishing a Session

Session Establishment involves creating a connection or interaction between two networked systems, allowing data exchange or communication. Sessions can be established using various protocols like TCP, UDP, SSH, HTTP, or FTP.

Process: Establishing a session involves initiating a connection, negotiating parameters (if needed), and establishing a communication channel between the systems involved.

These tools and concepts are essential in understanding network security, vulnerabilities, and methods used for network discovery, analysis, and establishing connections or sessions between systems. Always ensure ethical and legal use of these tools within authorized contexts.

Practice Question and Answers

1. What is the primary goal of SQL Injection attacks on web applications?

A. Gaining unauthorized access to databases

B. Disrupting server performance

C. Executing code on the user's browser

D. Intercepting network traffic

Answer: A. Gaining unauthorized access to databases

Explanation: SQL Injection attacks aim to manipulate SQL queries to gain unauthorized access to databases and extract sensitive information.

2. How does Cross-Site Scripting (XSS) typically impact web applications?

A. Modifying session cookies

B. Exploiting server misconfigurations

C. Executing malicious scripts on users' browsers

D. Intercepting database transactions

Answer: C. Executing malicious scripts on users' browsers

Explanation: XSS attacks inject and execute scripts on users' browsers, compromising their session or stealing information.

3. What vulnerability does Parameter/Form Tampering exploit in web applications?

A. Exploiting server-side validation

B. Altering hidden form fields or parameters

C. Encrypting sensitive data

D. Injecting malicious scripts

Answer: B. Altering hidden form fields or parameters

Explanation: Parameter/Form Tampering involves modifying hidden form fields or parameters to alter application behavior or gain unauthorized access.

4. What is the primary concern of Cookie/Session Poisoning attacks on web applications?

A. Encrypting session tokens

B. Manipulating or stealing session data

C. Exploiting server-side vulnerabilities

D. Executing code on the server

Answer: B. Manipulating or stealing session data

Explanation: Cookie/Session Poisoning involves tampering with cookies or session data to gain unauthorized access or perform malicious actions.

5. How does Error Message Interception affect web application security?

A. Modifying server configurations

B. Providing sensitive information to attackers

C. Intercepting user authentication

D. Disrupting server performance

Answer: B. Providing sensitive information to attackers

Explanation: Error Message Interception provides attackers with sensitive information useful for launching further attacks.

6. Which attack aims to manipulate URLs or hidden fields in web forms to alter application behavior?

A. Buffer Overflow

B. SQL Injection

C. Parameter/Form Tampering

D. Cross-Site Scripting (XSS)

Answer: C. Parameter/Form Tampering

Explanation: Parameter/Form Tampering involves modifying hidden fields or parameters in web forms to alter application behavior.

7. What risk does Buffer Overflow pose to web applications?

A. Intercepting network traffic

B. Disrupting server performance

C. Executing arbitrary code

D. Manipulating session cookies

Answer: C. Executing arbitrary code

Explanation: Buffer Overflow attacks aim to inject and execute malicious code by overflowing allocated memory buffers.

8. What is the primary objective of a Cross-Site Request Forgery (CSRF) attack on web applications?

A. Gaining unauthorized access to databases

B. Executing code on users' browsers

C. Hijacking user sessions to perform actions

D. Intercepting server responses

Answer: C. Hijacking user sessions to perform actions

Explanation: CSRF attacks exploit authenticated user sessions to perform unauthorized actions on behalf of the victim.

9. How does Cross-Site Request Forgery (CSRF) differ from Cross-Site Scripting (XSS)?

A. CSRF manipulates user inputs, while XSS executes malicious scripts in browsers

B. XSS hijacks user sessions, while CSRF exploits server vulnerabilities

C. XSS exploits form fields, while CSRF steals session cookies

D. CSRF exploits authentication, while XSS steals sensitive data

Answer: A. CSRF manipulates user inputs, while XSS executes malicious scripts in browsers

Explanation: CSRF tricks a user's browser into performing unintended actions, while XSS injects and executes malicious scripts.

10. What vulnerability might be exploited in a web application to execute arbitrary code by overflowing memory buffers?

A. SQL Injection

B. Buffer Overflow

C. Cross-Site Scripting (XSS)

D. Parameter/Form Tampering

Answer: B. Buffer Overflow

Explanation: Buffer Overflow attacks aim to inject and execute arbitrary code by overflowing allocated memory buffers.

11. What vulnerability does SQL Injection exploit in web applications?

A. Exploiting server-side validation

B. Altering hidden form fields or parameters

C. Manipulating database queries

D. Intercepting network traffic

Answer: C. Manipulating database queries

Explanation: SQL Injection attacks manipulate SQL queries executed by a web application to gain unauthorized access to databases.

12. How does Cross-Site Scripting (XSS) impact users interacting with a web application?

A. Executing code on the server

B. Altering hidden form fields

C. Modifying database records

D. Executing malicious scripts on users' browsers

Answer: D. Executing malicious scripts on users' browsers

Explanation: XSS attacks inject and execute malicious scripts in users' browsers, compromising their session or stealing information.

13. What risk does Parameter/Form Tampering pose to web applications?

A. Intercepting network traffic

B. Manipulating or altering form parameters

C. Exploiting server-side vulnerabilities

D. Encrypting sensitive data

Answer: B. Manipulating or altering form parameters

Explanation: Parameter/Form Tampering involves modifying hidden form fields or parameters to alter application behavior or gain unauthorized access.

14. What is the primary concern of Cookie/Session Poisoning attacks on web applications?

A. Encrypting session tokens

B. Manipulating or stealing session data

C. Exploiting server-side vulnerabilities

D. Intercepting database transactions

Answer: B. Manipulating or stealing session data

Explanation: Cookie/Session Poisoning involves tampering with cookies or session data to gain unauthorized access or perform malicious actions.

15. How does Error Message Interception impact web application security?

A. Modifying server configurations

B. Providing sensitive information to attackers

C. Intercepting user authentication

D. Disrupting server performance

Answer: B. Providing sensitive information to attackers

Explanation: Error Message Interception provides attackers with sensitive information useful for launching further attacks.

16. Which attack aims to manipulate URLs or hidden fields in web forms to alter application behavior?

A. Buffer Overflow

B. SQL Injection

C. Parameter/Form Tampering

D. Cross-Site Scripting (XSS)

Answer: C. Parameter/Form Tampering

Explanation: Parameter/Form Tampering involves modifying hidden fields or parameters in web forms to alter application behavior.

17. What risk does Buffer Overflow pose to web applications?

A. Intercepting network traffic

B. Disrupting server performance

C. Executing arbitrary code

D. Manipulating session cookies

Answer: C. Executing arbitrary code

Explanation: Buffer Overflow attacks aim to inject and execute malicious code by overflowing allocated memory buffers.

18. What is the primary objective of a Cross-Site Request Forgery (CSRF) attack on web applications?

A. Gaining unauthorized access to databases

B. Executing code on users' browsers

C. Hijacking user sessions to perform actions

D. Intercepting server responses

Answer: C. Hijacking user sessions to perform actions

Explanation: CSRF attacks exploit authenticated user sessions to perform unauthorized actions on behalf of the victim.

19. How does Cross-Site Request Forgery (CSRF) differ from Cross-Site Scripting (XSS)?

A. CSRF manipulates user inputs, while XSS executes malicious scripts in browsers

B. XSS hijacks user sessions, while CSRF exploits server vulnerabilities

C. XSS exploits form fields, while CSRF steals session cookies

D. CSRF exploits authentication, while XSS steals sensitive data

Answer: A. CSRF manipulates user inputs, while XSS executes malicious scripts in browsers

Explanation: CSRF tricks a user's browser into performing unintended actions, while XSS injects and executes malicious scripts.

20. What vulnerability might be exploited in a web application to execute arbitrary code by overflowing memory buffers?

A. SQL Injection

B. Buffer Overflow

C. Cross-Site Scripting (XSS)

D. Parameter/Form Tampering

Answer: B. Buffer Overflow

Explanation: Buffer Overflow attacks aim to inject and execute arbitrary code by overflowing allocated memory buffers.

21. What is the primary goal of an SQL Injection attack in web applications?

A. Intercepting server responses

B. Gaining unauthorized access to databases

C. Executing code on users' browsers

D. Altering hidden form fields

Answer: B. Gaining unauthorized access to databases

Explanation: SQL Injection aims to manipulate SQL queries to gain unauthorized access to databases and extract sensitive information.

22. How does Cross-Site Scripting (XSS) impact user interactions with web applications?

A. Modifying server configurations

B. Intercepting network traffic

C. Executing malicious scripts on users' browsers

D. Exploiting authentication vulnerabilities

Answer: C. Executing malicious scripts on users' browsers

Explanation: XSS attacks inject and execute malicious scripts in users' browsers, compromising their session or stealing information.

23. What risk does Parameter/Form Tampering pose to web applications?

A. Intercepting network traffic

B. Manipulating or altering form parameters

C. Exploiting server-side vulnerabilities

D. Encrypting sensitive data

Answer: B. Manipulating or altering form parameters

Explanation: Parameter/Form Tampering involves modifying hidden form fields or parameters to alter application behavior or gain unauthorized access.

24. What is the primary concern of Cookie/Session Poisoning attacks on web applications?

A. Exploiting server-side vulnerabilities

B. Manipulating or stealing session data

C. Intercepting database transactions

D. Encrypting session tokens

Answer: B. Manipulating or stealing session data

Explanation: Cookie/Session Poisoning involves tampering with cookies or session data to gain unauthorized access or perform malicious actions.

25. How does Error Message Interception impact web application security?

A. Modifying server configurations

B. Providing sensitive information to attackers

C. Intercepting user authentication

D. Disrupting server performance

Answer: B. Providing sensitive information to attackers

Explanation: Error Message Interception provides attackers with sensitive information useful for launching further attacks.

26. Which attack aims to manipulate URLs or hidden fields in web forms to alter application behavior?

A. Buffer Overflow

B. SQL Injection

C. Parameter/Form Tampering

D. Cross-Site Scripting (XSS)

Answer: C. Parameter/Form Tampering

Explanation: Parameter/Form Tampering involves modifying hidden fields or parameters in web forms to alter application behavior.

27. What risk does Buffer Overflow pose to web applications?

A. Disrupting server performance

B. Intercepting network traffic

C. Executing arbitrary code

D. Manipulating session cookies

Answer: C. Executing arbitrary code

Explanation: Buffer Overflow attacks aim to inject and execute malicious code by overflowing allocated memory buffers.

28. What is the primary objective of a Cross-Site Request Forgery (CSRF) attack on web applications?

A. Gaining unauthorized access to databases

B. Executing code on users' browsers

C. Hijacking user sessions to perform actions

D. Intercepting server responses

Answer: C. Hijacking user sessions to perform actions

Explanation: CSRF attacks exploit authenticated user sessions to perform unauthorized actions on behalf of the victim.

29. How does Cross-Site Request Forgery (CSRF) differ from Cross-Site Scripting (XSS)?

A. CSRF manipulates user inputs, while XSS executes malicious scripts in browsers

B. XSS hijacks user sessions, while CSRF exploits server vulnerabilities

C. XSS exploits form fields, while CSRF steals session cookies

D. CSRF exploits authentication, while XSS steals sensitive data

Answer: A. CSRF manipulates user inputs, while XSS executes malicious scripts in browsers

Explanation: CSRF tricks a user's browser into performing unintended actions, while XSS injects and executes malicious scripts.

30. What vulnerability might be exploited in a web application to execute arbitrary code by overflowing memory buffers?

A. SQL Injection

B. Buffer Overflow

C. Cross-Site Scripting (XSS)

D. Parameter/Form Tampering

Answer: B. Buffer Overflow

Explanation: Buffer Overflow attacks aim to inject and execute arbitrary code by overflowing allocated memory buffers.

Conclusion

In the realm of cybersecurity, the landscape is ever-evolving, and the importance of securing web applications cannot be overstated. This book has delved into the intricate world of web application vulnerabilities, exploits, and the measures essential for fortifying against potential threats.

We've explored the arsenal of attacks, from SQL Injection to Cross-Site Scripting (XSS), Parameter/Form Tampering, and more. Each of these attacks underscores the critical need for robust security practices in web application development.

Understanding these vulnerabilities empowers developers, security professionals, and enthusiasts to preemptively mitigate risks and fortify applications against malicious intrusions. The responsibility falls not only on developers but on every stakeholder involved in the software development lifecycle to uphold security as a priority.

Moreover, this book has highlighted the significance of continuous vigilance and staying updated with emerging threats and evolving security practices. Regular audits, robust input validation, secure coding practices, and leveraging tools to detect vulnerabilities are vital pillars in this ongoing battle against cyber threats.

As we conclude this journey through the intricacies of hacking web applications, the takeaway is clear: Security must be ingrained into the foundation of every web application, ensuring resilience against potential exploits and safeguarding sensitive user data.

Remember, the quest for security is a perpetual endeavor. Embrace it, refine it, and together, let's fortify our digital world against the lurking threats.

Thank you for embarking on this educational journey with us. Stay vigilant, stay secure!